To the Mountains
Where time and life
Changes. A place w
friends become fri

Michael Dutch

Collector's Edition

Cowboy Poetry
The Gathering

Michael Whitaker

Foreword by
Alan Halvorson

Edited by Janice Coggin

Cowboy
Miner
PRODUCTIONS

Cowboy Poetry, The Gathering
Text and Song Lyrics © 2005 Michael Whitaker
Design and Layout Copyright © 2005 Cowboy Miner Productions
Edited by Janice Coggin

Publisher: Cowboy Miner Productions
P.O. Box 9674
Phoenix, AZ 85068
Phone: (602) 569-6063
www.CowboyMiner.com

Publisher's Cataloging-in-Publication Data
Whitaker, Michael, 1957—
Cowboy Poetry, The Gathering
Michael Whitaker. Foreword by Alan Halvorson.
Edited by Janice Coggin.
  p. cm. Illustrated.

  ISBN: 1-931725-12-8

1. Cowboy History—Poetry. 2. Cowboy Poetry—Montana.
3. Northwestern History (U.S.)—Poetry. 4. Poetry—Montana Historical.
5. Cowboy Poetry—Idaho.
  I. Title

Library of Congress Control Number: 2004115179

Book Design & Typesetting: SageBrush Publications, Tempe, Arizona
Jacket Design: ATG Productions, Phoenix, Arizona
Jacket Photo: Lauri Gallion
Printing: Bang Printing, Brainerd, Minnesota

Printed and bound in the United States of America

To my wife Judy and my wonderful children

Contents

Acknowledgments

It all started with my dad taking me up in the hills ridin' horses. We rode to some of the prettiest country that you could ever imagine. Spent nights on the ground and in cabins so tucked away that no one could ever find ya. I think of how young I was then, ridin' up trails that if ya met someone, forward and back is all that ya had, because up or down just wasn't an option.

My dad passed when I was eighteen years old. I think back at how short of time I really had with him and just how much he was able to show and teach me. It was pretty hard to lose someone like that. It was then that my dear ol' Uncle Bill Gallion stepped forward and took me under his wing. A few years back he stopped by for coffee and told me about a Cowboy Gathering he'd been to. He told me of the Cowboy Poetry and just how much he liked it. He knows me damn good, but didn't have a clue that I had been writin' most of my life. When I read him a few of my poems, needless to say he was surprised. The next summer he invited me to his Outfitter's Camp and introduced me to Alan Halvorson and Keven Inman. I soon started recitin' poems with them for the clients around the campfire. Since then I've been teamed up with Alan, Keven, Morry "Spiff" Walters, Padre Gregg McDonald and his dear and caring wife Carla. We are known as the "Tahoma Range Rhymers" and perform around the local area. So ya can see I owe a few folks for their helpin' hands and kindness.

Thanks ya all.

I would like to thank my ol' pard Paul Buol. He's a friend that all of us should have and he's the brother that I never had. Paul and I have traveled through Washington, Montana, Idaho and have seen some of the prettiest splendor that the good Lord could muster up.

I really owe Paul because he is the Guinea Pig that had to listen to the rough drafts. You wonder why he just didn't get up and leave? Well, can't say that I'm smart but I sure am a little cleaver. See, when you're in the mountains of Idaho, stuck in a tent and the outside temp is ten below, there's no place to run!

He's a good listener.

Thanks to all of my good friends who have supported me and learned to laugh at the right times. You're too kind.

Thanks to Melinda Walters, Sharon Buol, my son Nick Whitaker, Lauri Gallion and everyone who let me use their photographs in my poetry. I would like to give a special thanks to my brother-in-law, Mike Twardoski, whose photography has inspired many of my poems.

Also I need to thank my dear wife of twenty-three years. It's been such an enjoyable time sharin' life with someone that has the same sense of adventure as I do. I'm lucky to be with someone that faces change with the same optimism as me. I would also like to thank my children for all of their support. Nick for being a dictionary in tennis shoes, Will for bein' Will, the comedian of the family and Courtney for being the undeterred free spirit. I wish I could be like Courtney all of the time, instead of the throw back that I am.

I think my family is finally takin' me serious, it's been a spell since the phrase "mid-life crisis" has been muttered.

Thanks to each and everyone of you!

Brand of the Rockin' Diamond G Outfitters

Foreword

At the end of a long day's ride, the gathering at the evening campfire etched the day's events into an aural history that documented the day-to-day experience of the American cowboy. Mike Whitaker is following in the tradition of Western Verse that was born at the gathering. Verse that puts forward the history, the hopes, the dreams, the humor, the memories of events past as well as the good natured tall tales that reflect one man's journey through the western lifestyle.

I met Mike around the campfire at his uncle's outfit in the Cascade Mountains of Washington State. Uncle Bill runs a dude string and Mike provides the steak supper and campfire show. The dudes get the experience of a lifetime, a sore butt, a full stomach, and for dessert, tales reflecting the passion that one man has for relishing life cast in the hoofprints of a time gone by.

You'll find these reflections hit home like the time spent remembering your own trails.

Saddle up, head out and enjoy "The Gathering."

Alan Halvorson
April 24, 2004

My grandfather, Oscar Whitaker

Chapter 1
Old Saddles

Introduction

When putting my thoughts on paper, I discovered quite a few things about myself and others that I've come to know through the years. I have become somewhat more critical of myself, which is good on one hand and bad on the other. I have found that some of the people I know are actually interesting. It has taught me to take the time and listen to what folks have to say. I have a friend that has taken some of my poems and put them to song. The strange thing is that no one knew he could write music or, for that matter, sing. When I heard him playing one of my poems for the first time I about fell off my chair. You never know what people are really like until you take the time to listen.

I have always been the type that didn't care too much what people may think of me and in fact "didn't much give a damn." Well, I guess I do now. I write from what I see and hear. I write of everyday life, the past and present. I imagine the lives the cowboys had, back when things were tough and straightforward. Sometimes a poem may be five or six people all wrapped up in one. Usually the character is someone most of us have known, that cowboy that lives down the road, our dads, moms, or family. I write about the situation we get ourselves into and think that it only happens to us. I try to take simple things and leave them simple. I like music and have found that poetry is just a way to sing a song when you can't stand hearing yourself. I've tried writing music, some good, some bad, but have found that, for me, the nakedness of poetry is one of the greatest ways to get a thought across, that one on one you have with the listener. There was a moment when I was reciting a poem about my father who had passed away when I came eye to eye with a lady who had a small tear running down her cheek. I knew then that what I was doing had an impact on folks. If you can make them cry one moment and laugh the next, you know that you're on to something.

The folks that recite Western Verse and sing that old forgotten music, are a special breed. They are usually more interested in hearing your stories than tellin' their own.

I have been invited on a ride that has taken me to places that I couldn't even imagine. A ride I wish I could have started many years ago. I would like to thank the friends and strangers that I've really come to know, the fellow Cowboy Poets that have helped me get started and are honest in a manner that usually mothers only have. I have not found a way to say thanks until now. The biggest compliment I can give them would be to just carry on with what I'm doing and what I'm doing is writing, reciting and enjoying life. Hopefully a poem or two will strike a chord in your heart, kick up an old memory or just make you feel like taking a trip to Montana or Idaho to see some of the county I've seen and encounter a few of the folks I've met.

What lies ahead in this collection is some nonfiction, some semi-nonfiction and some just right out lies. Which are which?

Good luck, that's for you to figure out.

Hope you enjoy,

Mike Whitaker

Photo by Melinda Walter

Skip Gorman

The Gathering

They pulled the chuck wagon by the creek,
    unhitched and watered up the team.
Old Cooky he pulled out a couple pots
    and filled them from the stream.

The horses now unsaddled,
    they cut them loose to run the night.
A few boys watched the cattle,
    night herded to keep them right.

The sun faded behind the hills
    as the grub was being served.
The Cowboys a little quiet,
    not a solitary word.

Then a fiddle softy played a song.
    Sweet music filled the air.
He sang of home and yesterday.
    They pretended not to care.

Then one by one they gathered
    to hear this Cowboy sing.
Listen to the music
    and the memories that it did bring.

One by one they gathered,
    they listened through the night.
Staring at the fire,
    and the flickering of the light.

The music calms the cattle.
    The night herders hum the songs.
Thinking about those pretty girls,
    the ones they left back home.

Then the cattle gathered
    as if they knew the words he sang.
The Cowboys stared into the night
    wishin' they were home again.

When the days turn into weeks
    and the hills all look the same;
When the drive runs just a bit too long
    out on the open range—

When that Cowboy pulls his fiddle out,
    and he sings of long ago;
It is then the Cowboys gather,
    and reflect on days of old.

One by one they gather
    to listen to him play.
The fiddle fills the coulees
    at the ending of the day.

One by one they fall asleep,
    and the cattle settle down.
It is only then this fiddle player
    will lay his head upon the ground.

The Gathering

The life out on a cattle drive
    sometimes can take its toll.
It drains the spirit from the Cowboys,
    the young men to the old.

And that is why they gather,
    to listen to him sing.
To listen to his fiddle
    and the way he makes it ring.

One by one they gather
    and listen to him play.
Play songs of the homeland,
    a million miles away.

One by one they gather.

A Cold December Day

The frost lays across the ground
   and the moon hides behind the trees.
The trees stand bare and naked,
   at their feet a running stream.

The stream is cold as winter;
   the night now fades away.
The morning is like a painting
   on this cold December day.

Horses lift their heads up,
   make their way from off the ground.
The chill runs through their blood and hide,
   but they hardly make a sound.

The sky, it slowly lightens.
   The day is on its way.
Life has a new beginning
   on this cold December day.

He leads the horses one by one
   and loads up all the gear.
He casts his eyes up to the sky.
   It's the winter clouds he fears.

The Elk are grazin' up above.
   The air is more than cold.
Brushes ice from his old saddle,
   a familiar tale that's told.

A tale of a cowboy,
　　his life and simple ways.
Livin' life how he sees fit
　　on a cold December day.

Rides across the meadows
　　with a lead rope in his hand.
Life's a little hard at times,
　　but it's a life he understands.

The morning turns into a winter snow.
　　He can barely see.
It slowly starts to build up.
　　It stacks upon the trees.

The trail is now a white stripe
　　that winds on up the hill.
The wind a little stronger,
　　he feels this winter chill.

But it's a chill that he has felt before,
　　not a stranger to his hide.
So he heads on up the snow-white trail
　　running across the mountain side.

It's pretty in a strange way,
　　even though it's hard to bear.
He meanders through the mountains,
　　showing not a care.

But it's all this cowboy's ever known,
　　and it's all he ever will.
An old man and his ponies
　　ridin' across the snowy hills.

They say it was a winter storm,
    and it caught him by surprise.
They found his horses on their own,
    running across the mountain side.

They never tried to find him,
    for they knew it was his way.
Forever in the mountains
    on a cold "December day."

Photo by Lauri Gallion

Side Pork & Baked Beans

The ol' Dutch Oven is hangin' with ease,
  big chunks of side pork floatin' in beans.
Another is sittin' just off to the side.
  The gun powder biscuits are starting to rise.

The fire is perfect. The day was too long,
  a cowboy recites a workin' man's poem.
The jug makes its way around the fire with ease,
  just waitin' for biscuits, side pork and baked beans.

The bedrolls are scattered across the hard dusty ground.
  The meal is now finished they soon will be found.
The night is lit up with the stars from the sky.
  The Cowboys now settle as the coyotes do cry.

Life as a cowboy is usually short lived,
  Their day-to-day livin' doesn't have much to give.
It's the life they do live, too hard it may seem.
  Punchin' and drivin' is a workin' man's dream.

The high country ground is too rocky and steep,
  not a flat spot for miles, you'd best sleep on your feet.
The hot desert ground is too soft and too flat.
  The wind blows so hard you'd best screw down your hat.

Sore cracked ol' fingers and achin' ol' backs—
    in the blistering heat the sweat builds under your hat.
Thirst that would drive most men insane,
    the life of the Cowboy on the wide open range.

The fire is perfect. The day was too long,
    A cowboy recites a workin' man's poem.
The jug makes it way around the fire with ease
    just waitin' for biscuits side pork and baked beans.

Saddle 'em Up

G   C
The cattle are grazin' on the high upper range.
    D   G
The ranch lies in the valley where the wind has been tamed.

     G   C
The spring rains have helped, the summer survive.
    D   G
The cattle look good and should bring a good price.

D   G
So saddle 'em up boys, head up the hill.
    D   G
Head to the high range where the dogies are still.

    G   C
Still eatin' high pastures, let 'em fatten up nice.
    D   G
The cattle look good and should bring a good price.

A good year was needed, it's been quite a spell.
It's been almost forever since the beef prices fell.

But ranchin' is known to have no guarantees.
You can stay if you wish. You can leave if you please.

So saddle 'em up boys, head up the hill.
Head to the high range where the dogies are still.

Still eatin' high pastures 'til the northern snow blows.
Been ranchin' forever. It's all that we know.

Why can't every year be sunny and green,
Where the cattle are fat and there's a full runnin' stream?

The sweet grass knee high where the cattle are found.
The dogies all scattered across the high pasture ground.

So saddle 'em up boys, push 'em on down.
Down the long rolling hills and the steep rocky ground.

Run 'em on down where ol' pappy does lie;
Over his grave to see the look in his eye.

Don't dilly-dally, the price is just right.
So saddle 'em up, it'll be whiskey tonight.

Remember this day, there are so very few.
It will always be known as the time we once knew.

So saddle 'em up boys, head up the hill.
Head to the high range where the dogies are still.

Still eatin' high pastures, let 'em fatten up nice.
The cattle look good and should bring a good price.

Now the high range is empty, the cattle are gone.
All that is left is a cold winter's song.

The green turns to white, the sun turns to snow.
Been ranchin' forever, it's all that we know.

The Gathering

So settle on down boys, winter is here.
The white moon is shinin', the cold sky is clear.

Take a load off your feet and rest for a while.
The fire is hot, there's more wood in the pile.

So dream of the year when the price was so high.
The cowboys all smirked, had a look in their eye.

When ranchin' was good, at least for a spell.
A time to remember, a story to tell.

So saddle 'em up boys, head up the hill.
Head to the high range where dogies are still.

Still grazin' high pastures in the hot summer sun.
Ride high in your saddle, 'til your days work is done.

Ride high in your saddle, 'til your days work is done.

Music and Lyrics by Michael Whitaker

Morning Bells

The creek stumbles cross the rocks.
Morning light is still afar.
The young cowboy saddles a blazed-face horse
Beneath the morning stars.

A wrangler's job he honors.
Across the creek and then
He rides out through the darkness
To bring them ponies in.

He caps the ridge and breaks on down,
A coulee just below.
He pulls the blaze up to a stop
Beneath the moon aglow.

He listens, oh, so carefully
The sounds so far and faint.
The dark horses hide within the night.
He spots a shining paint.

Then morning bells fill the air,
The horses just ahead.
He guides them towards the wagons.
The cowboys rise from bed.

The bells around the old mare's neck,
They play a wranglers tune.
The morning sun fills up the day.
He no longer feels the moon.

Horses come a runnin',
Slide as they make camp.
The morning bells aringin';
The horses do their dance.

Morning bells do fill the air
When a wrangler starts his day.
The young wrangler has done his job.
He now has earned his stay.

This wrangler is the youngest.
His jobs don't match the rest.
He works out on the range,
And some day he'll be the best.

But he has something that the cowboys don't—
A story he can tell.
Life don't get much better
When it starts with morning bells.

The horses in the darkness,
The sound of hooves ahead,
The morning bells do waken
The cowboys from their beds.

The run across the meadows,
The bells swing side to side.
The wrangler's on a blaze-faced horse
Trailin' right behind.

They say the bells stay with you,
And sometimes within the night,
You can hear the bells a ringin'
Right before daylight.

Too many years before my time—
Just a story that I tell
Of a wrangler on a blazed-face horse
And the sound of morning bells.

Something About Mornin'

There's somethin' about mornin' that's hard to explain.
  It's a time when the world stands still,
Right before daylight tries to make its claim.
  Life is calm and oh, so real.

Coffee tastes better, the air's a bit more pure,
  the night has nowhere to hide.
There's somethin' about mornin' that's hard to explain,
  just waitin' to see the sunrise.

There's somethin' about ridin' way back in the hills
  to a place where nobody goes.
The elk just a grazin' until they get their fill
  and the tops are still covered with snow.

The lakes are blue, as blue dares to get,
  the trees are all weathered like me.
There's somethin' about ridin' way back in the hills.
  It's a place where I would rather be.

There's somethin' about sleepin' under the stars,
  the heavens lookin' down on you.
When you are high in the hills the stars are a bit brighter,
  and the night is a bit deeper than blue.

The cool mountain air numbs your weathered ol' face.
  The sounds of the night move around.
There's somethin' about sleepin' under the stars,
  the best sleep that I have ever found.

There's somethin' about a campfire when you are out alone,
    somehow it becomes a close friend.
It takes the chill off your face and your shoulders,
    at times it can make your soul mend.

The fire does flicker against the trees and the rocks.
    The wood makes a cracklin' sound.
There's somethin' about a campfire, when you are out all alone.
    It's a friend when no one's around.

There's somethin' about livin' the way that I do.
    It's so simple, it doesn't take too much mind.
The pace a bit slower, now I am a bit older,
    disappointment is real hard to find.

The mornin's are peaceful, the coffee tastes good.
    The stars shine over the fire each night.
But there's somethin' about mornin' that is hard to explain,
    just waitin' to see the sunrise.

Desert Wind

The wind blew across this forbidden land,
    the dust was powder dry.
The ground was scattered with sage and rock.
    The hills they touched the sky.

Across this country all alone
    it was a shame I could not share.
It took me to a place in time,
    back a hundred years.

It had a sure and certain beauty
    words never could describe.
Taking in the colors
    from this desert mountainside.

Then suddenly, like a dream,
    I could hear this ghostly sound.
The wind would make it come and go,
    I could feel it in the ground.

What direction was a mystery.
    The sound was wild and untamed.
This sound kept just out of sight,
    uncertain and so strange.

Then it broke out like a tidal wave.
    Above me they all ran.
Horses of many colors
    blending with the land.

The Gathering

Stopping from a full-out run,
    they turned and looked at me.
Some how not fearing danger,
    showing pride and dignity.

The lead horse pawed at the ground,
    throwing dust upon his back.
His presence stood above the rest.
    His hide was coral black.

Then in a wink of an old man's eye
    down the hill these horses ran.
Over the side of this desert slope
    that is too desolate for man.

I could hear the thunder miles away.
    It was a long and a steady roar.
I sat there until the sun went down.
    I could not hear them any more.

What I saw that day
    was only just a dream.
A herd of wild horses
    running across a desert scene.

A water color memory
    that is painted in my mind.
A herd of wild horses
    running through the book of time.

Mountain Storm

The snow capped mountains turn black as night,
    though it is the middle of the day.
The storm rolls in low and strong,
    the trees begin to sway.

The air turns cold and heavy.
    You could cut it with a knife.
I settle down to watch the show
    as the day turns into night.

The clouds turn blacker than midnight,
    electricity is in the air.
I can feel it run across my skin,
    up my neck and through my hair.

Then the lightenin' strikes too close to us.
    The thunder shakes the ground.
I watch the clouds for another strike,
    I fear that deadly sound.

My horse pulls heavy on the reins,
    they are cutting through my hands.
I settle him down once again.
    It is more than he can stand.

The hail pounds down like a shotgun blast.
    We both tuck our heads down tight.
The sky turns loose with another round,
    it is loud and, oh, so bright.

It pounds and pops for an eternity,
    then slowly drifts away.
The sky starts to lighten up.
    The night turns into day.

The sun comes out once again.
    The trees begin to steam.
The fog rolls across the valley.
    It creates a hazy dream.

Times like this reminds me
    of just who is in control.
There is nothing like a "Mountain Storm"
    to shake your very soul.

Photo by Pat Dean

Out Of Time

He's tall and skinny, as skinny can get.
His face is dried like a prune.
To bed at seven and up at three-thirty,
he's been up a full day by noon.

He bought his pick-up right out of the showroom,
but that was in sixty-eight.
Now instead of ridin', he just sits and watches
as a bronc busts out of the gate.

No time for BS, just give it to him straight.
A short answer is what you'll get.
One eye squints like he's tryin' to listen.
It's just the smoke from his cigarette.

He almost got married, but that was years back.
Had to go, he was runnin' behind.
Always liked kids in their oversized hats,
but he never found the time.

He makes a small livin' shoein' horses.
His back's about to give in.
His dog has a limp from a too-close encounter,
a horse a bit faster then him.

His boots are cracked, his hat's old and stained,
    his Wrangler's drag on the ground.
He wishes he could ride, like he did once before,
    but his youth is nowhere to be found.

He's tall and skinny, as skinny can get,
    a dog and a beat up ol' truck.
He's a wore-out ol' cowboy with nothin' to show,
    a buckin' horse rider that's ran out of luck.

A Cowboy's Way

Conversation is not his preferable trait.
　　He's hard and cold at heart.
He wakes long before the mornin' shows,
　　and the day comes to a start.

Saddles up long before the dawn,
　　and in the dark he rides away.
Most don't understand him,
　　as he lives life a different way.

Ol' Joe watches him as he rides away
　　in the cold mornin' air.
Pays not much attention,
　　gives a shrug as if he doesn't care.

The lights within the bunk house
　　now burn across the porch.
Ol' Joe has breakfast waitin',
　　the outside a little scorched.

But the Cowboys don't complain much,
　　it's the best life that they've found.
This ranch is owned by honest folk,
　　the best there is around.

An honest day for honest pay,
　　jobs are very few.
The Cowboys life is changin'
　　from the time that they once knew.

The Gathering

They head out as the sun does crest
    atop the desert hills.
They head on down the river
    where the cattle eat and mill.

The cattle are awaiting,
    for the sale that ends the year.
Then they spot that ornery ranch boss,
    which means the cattle's near.

They take a course right at him,
    and he snips as they ride up.
Scours at them and points the way
    like they're stupid and just screwed up.

But most have gotten used to him,
    his unforgiving ways.
Just a drover's job that lets them
    live a life from yesterday.

They round 'em up head 'em home,
    before the sun goes down.
Put 'em in the holdin' pens,
    clean up and head to town.

The half pay now awaits them,
    because the cattle are corralled.
The best hats sit upon their heads,
    and they no longer smell so foul.

But their yahoos only last a night,
    'cause the drive now surely waits.
Their destination is a little far,
    half across this endless state.

They have a day to rest up
    before the journey does begin.
A cattle drive from nowhere,
    and somewhere will be the end.

The chuck wagon is now loaded up,
    and the Cowboys are sittin' tall.
The gates are flung wide open,
    and the ranch boss, he yells his call.

The ranch now seems so lonely,
    and the year now has an end.
The quietness is eerie,
    you can hear it in the wind.

Then across the river and to the top
    the desert stretches out of sight.
The dust billows like a whirlwind,
    and the day turns into night.

They stop when the sun goes down,
    a little wore out, a little tired.
Joe, he pulls out the pots and pans,
    the ranch boss builds a fire.

The Gathering

Old Joe now cooks up supper.
    He serves corn bread and beans.
The Cowboys' eyes cross from fear
    when the eatin' is so lean.

The turns are shared for herdin'
    as the night sky shines with stars.
Just the start of a cattle drive
    that runs a bit too far.

A week has passed and the stockyard
    is comin' into sight.
The Cowboys now sittin' tall
    and feelin' mighty right.

The cattle are corralled up,
    and the Cowboys make their way.
Cheyenne is quite a site to see,
    not too bad of a place to stay.

The whiskey and the women
    are plentiful they do find.
Just trying to take their money
    and the days they've left behind.

But the ranch boss's a little smarter
    than the Cowboys on that day.
See, he makes them wait a day or two
    before they draw their pay.

Some head down to Denver.
  Some they stay awhile.
Some head off to Nebraska
  where they ride for miles and miles.

Some turn around with Ol' Joe
  and that boss they can not bear
Back across Wyoming,
  just to breathe some mountain air.

But one thing that is for sure,
  they will be back one more time.
'Cause when you are a Cowboy
  there ain't much more that you can find.

Some say that Ol' Joe needs cookin' lessons,
  and that ranch boss could use a smile.
Some say that there must be a stockyard
  within a hundred miles.

But the pay is right, and the Cowboy life
  does bring them back each year.
A steady job and a family
  is somethin' that they fear.

Now Ol' Joe he pulls the checkers out.
  That ranch boss stares at him.
Not a word is ever spoken,
  somehow these two are friends.

Another year has ended,
    and winter comes in slow.
Life has turned another page.
    It's the only life they know.

This way of life that they once knew
    now is found within a book.
A hard and ornery ranch boss
    and an open-fire cook.

Whisky Creek

We went for a high country ride
    where the air is crisp and clear.
We hadn't been up to these parts
    for nearly twenty years.

The same ol' rocks were sittin' there—
    they hadn't moved an inch.
Forgot the trail was so damn steep,
    hopped down and cranked the cinch.

The snow was just a little high,
    but the view hadn't changed one bit.
Finally made it to the top of the hill,
    went to setup by the crick.

But there seemed to be a problem,
    one we never had before.
The crick that once ran all year long
    wasn't runnin' anymore.

I knew the summer was a little dry,
    I knew it hadn't rained.
But I figured that a crick like this
    would be runnin' just the same.

Our camp cook looked a little thin.
    See, he decided to modernize.
Instead of spuds and bacon,
    to save weight he'd brought freeze-dried.

But the first meal went down real good
    even though it was a little risky.
Instead of a quart of water
    he replaced it with some whiskey.

It wasn't exactly perfect.
    It went down purt' near the same.
The taste was a little different,
    But I heard no one complain.

So we went further up the mountainside
    In search of a runnin' crick.
We looked high and low for a crick that flowed.
    Our ol' cook was lookin' sick.

So one more time with whiskey
    our freeze-dried now was served.
The taste was wearin' a little thin.
    but I never heard a single word.

So further up the mountainside,
    in search of runnin' water.
We looked high and low for a crick that flowed.
    Now we were gettin' a little bothered.

We made it to the snow line.
    We filled our pots and pans.
We built us a big ol' fire
    for meltin' snow and warmin' hands.

We pulled out the freeze-dried once again,
   now it was water that we used.
But we had a little problem—
   See, now we're out of booze

The next morning down the hill we went.
   We cut our ride a little short.
We were all in desperation
   for a rib steak and a snort.

I guess there is a moral here,
   a thought we'd like to share;
Make sure the cricks are runnin'—
   as for whiskey, bring a spare.

Trails End

The rocks and the cliffs hang over his head.
    The river winds all day long.
The sound of the hoofs hittin' the trail,
    the wind sings its seasonal song.

A buck bust up from off of the river
    just gettin' his morning drink.
Mountains so high the tops he can't see,
    time so slow it makes a man think.

The mules hang their heads as they wind down the trail
    a bit bothered by the cool mountain air.
By darkness his ride should be at its end.
    They all are showing some wear.

The bed at the cabin is as soft as a feather.
    It's just what this cowboy does need.
He's not fond of the ground for nights on end.
    His age is showing ya see.

The warmth and the shelter the cabin does lend,
    heals his body and mind.
A potbelly stove on a cool mountain evening
    will suit this ol' Cowboy just fine.

The winters get longer as time passes by.
    The summers seem shorter each year.
They say an old cowboy has wisdom to spare.
    If that's so, then why is he here.

This life on the trail gets just a bit harder.
    It's the only thing this ol' boy knows.
The mountains and him have become quite a pair.
    Somehow it became his home.

When he's dead and gone no one will notice
    or ever give him much mind.
I am not really sure what heaven will offer,
    If it's like this, it will suit him just fine.

The Gathering

Photo by Lauri Gallion

Trail's End

A Quiet Understanding

They say that when he was young
  this gift first came to light.
He always hung by the corral
  watching mysteries unfold.

He watched until the sun went down
  and day turned into night.
Now he works with wild horses,
  the ones so strong and bold.

His tools are somewhat simple.
  His life is simple, too.
A round corral, a foot of dust,
  he slips on his leather gloves.

His work is based upon his life,
  an old hat and wore out boots.
Now age has slowly changed him.
  An untamed horse is what he loves.

Hard cases they do send him.
  He thinks a lot like them.
The ones that folks don't understand,
  spirits still untamed.

The Gathering

He doesn't try to change them,
    just learns to be their friend.
He knows just what they're all about.
    Their thoughts are just the same.

He snubs them to show control,
    he looks them in the eye.
The horses will fades away.
    He loosens up the rope.

Slow and small he approaches them,
    calm and, oh, so shy.
His way and all his manners,
    a trust that comes so slow.

Then a bond emerges,
    an understanding has been found.
The ground work slowly happens,
    the two now work as one.

The spirit shows once again,
    now controlled with little sound.
It's not a game of winners,
    they both have surely won.

A circle he now paces,
    the gentle swinging rope.
Not a word has been spoken,
    just a long and steady eye.

The glances are now many.
  The horse circles eyeing hope.
The horse now stops,
  turns his way and blows a sheepish sigh.

The cowboy kneels on he ground,
  the horse moves his way.
Sniffs his shirt and stares at him
  with eyes that understand.

Now understanding has been found,
  a bond that's sure to stay.
The first small step of many,
  the love of horse and man.

Cowboy Poet

The morning sun warms up the air
   left over from the night.
Shadows from the canyons
   now are filled with morning light.

He gets upon his tired feet,
   stokes the withered fire.
Fills the pot up one more time,
   his bones are cold and tired.

Throws the saddle on the back
   of the horse he's rode for years.
All the Cowboys mount up,
   ride through the canyons steep and shear.

They push the cattle along the trail,
   the one that has no end.
They know what they are there for,
   it's the cattle they must tend.

The dust and heat surrounds the day.
   Another day or two must pass.
Then they will have made their way,
   to where the cattle turn to cash.

But when the day comes to an end,
   the cool night sneaks around.
With stars a hangin', the fire bright,
   it's when you hear that lonesome sound.

The mood, a tad bit somber,
   the stares and thoughts run deep.
That old cowboy tells a tale or two
   until they're fast a sleep.

Rhyming words from what he's seen
   brings the world to life.
He tells his tales and rhymes his words
   far into the night.

He pulls the blanket across his shoulders.
   He tilts his hat across his eyes.
The Cowboys and the cattle
   are now still and oh so quiet.

He dreams of a life much better,
   a new way far from here.
He seems to come back to this way of life
   each and every year.

Some they just don't know him,
   some don't even know his name.
Some say he was an outlaw,
   but they like him just the same.

But he is just a Cowboy,
   his life is pushin' herds.
But at night you can hear him tellin' tales
   and rhymin' simple words.

With all the cattle sold off,
 to the saloon the Cowboys head.
But he slips upon his pony
 He rides away instead.

They spot him in the distance.
 They grin for it's his way.
They listen as he spins a verse,
 they hope to meet again someday.

Photo by Melinda Walter

Skip Gorman

Hillside Serenade

Stumbled down a hillside,
    see, my horse had come up lame.
Below I heard a cowboy
    singin' across the open plains.

The evenin' sun was settin'.
    It was low upon the ground.
He sat there by a desert fire.
    There was no one else around.

He yodeled with his chin up high
    in the desert sky.
He sang so sad the yeller moon
    soon began to cry.

He never had a single clue
    that I sat there upon that hill.
I wished that I could sing like him,
    but I know I never will.

His voice was soft as southern silk,
    his manner runs out slow.
He sat alone in cow camp
    singin' songs of Little Joe.

He sang songs of the wranglers,
    the strife they had to bear.
His songs are like a feather
    floating through the desert air.

His music has been his life.
    His voice has been his ride.
His fiddle rang through the air,
    you could hear the coyotes cry.

History fills this Cowboy's soul.
    He tells his lessons well.
I sat there on that desert night.
    My eyes began to swell.

I listened to his music
    and all the stories that it told.
Cowboy Skip a singin'
    of a time long, long ago.

To my ol' pard "Skip Gorman"

Swallerin' Pride

Tabacky was a way of life when I was just a kid.
Some came in a big ol' plug, some others had a lid.
I've seen 'em go a whole darn day and never spit a lick.
I knew that I wanted some, but I knew it'd make me sick.

One day this ol' boy looked at me and put his can my way.
I stood there like I saw a ghost, didn't know just what to say.
When the Cowboys started chucklin' it was time to be a man.
I eyed 'em like a fightin' dog, I reached and grabbed that can.

I popped that ol' lid open. I took 'er three fingers deep.
It lined those rosy lips of mine and floated 'cross my teeth.
I turned and looked 'em in the eye—nothin' to this stuff.
My head she started spinnin', started tanglin' with the snuff.

My legs got a little shaky. My ears was burnin' hot.
My nose she was a runnin'. I started drippin' snot.
Spittin' was against my will, I pulled hard against my collar.
The only option I had left was just to up and swaller.

I gave a mighty gulp that day. I finally got her down.
But this is when I saw the light. I quickly turned around.
I headed for a big ol' tree. I puked, and moaned and gagged.
The Cowboys just a cuttin' loose as I hugged that big ol' snag.

I think I lurned my lessin, little green to be a man.
I'd rather tame a rattlin' snake, than tabacky in a can.

Long Day Ahead

The old windup clock rings next to his head.
   His eyes open one by one.
The fire has died. His shoulders are cold,
   no sign of the morning sun.

His pants are stiff from yesterday's mud
   on the bottoms of these wore out jeans.
The coffee is brewing. His mind starts to clear.
   A new life would be better it seems.

Strolls out to feed the horses and mules
   some hay and a bucket of oats.
The bray and the knickers fill up the cool morning.
   He might put on a heavier coat.

Fixed up some breakfast, bacon and egg.
   It suits this ol' Cowboy just fine.
The sun slowly rises, a gentle reminder,
   best get movin' 'cause he's losing time.

Gears up the string, loads up the boxes,
   checks the loads, one by one.
He heads 'em on out down through the long winding canyon,
   gets a face full of the morning sun.

The morning is purty but winter is coming.
   The mornings a bit colder each day.
The wind starts to blow, the clouds start to thicken,
   tree tops are starting to sway.

The Gathering

Hopes that the snow holds off for a bit,
    twenty more miles to go.
He's never had luck with weather or women.
    It quietly starts to snow.

Pulls down his hat, turns up his collar,
    the ears on his horse are laid back.
He turns his neck to check on the mules.
    Now the snow has covered the packs.

The sky starts to darken, the day's at its end.
    The ranch is barely in sight.
The light from the lantern fills up the windows.
    The day has now turned into night.

Rides in the barn out of the weather,
    unloads and puts the riggin' away.
Supper now waits, the cookin' smells good,
    a nice ending to a long day.

Talks for a bit, but knows where he's headed,
    to a big ol' feather bed.
Gives thanks for the meal, but he best get restin',
    he's got a long, long day ahead.

Red Rock Passage

The shadows long upon the day,
    the day slows to an end.
The end of a survival,
    survival of horse and man.

Man not fit for steep rock cliffs,
    rock cliffs that shape their way.
Their way within the shadows,
    the shadows long upon the day.

The night is overwhelming,
    overwhelming with desert sounds.
Sounds echo through the red rock cliffs,
    rocks and moonlight abound.

Abound is the red rock beauty,
    the beauty fills this land.
Land of the survival,
    not fit for horse or man.

The night is filled with desert stars,
    stars cast across the sky.
The sky as deep as the canyons,
    canyons filled with desert cries.

Cries of coyotes linger,
    linger through the desert night.
The night now fills the canyons.
    The canyons are softened with moonlight.

The Gathering

Time owns this land of red rock cliffs,
  a reminder of who we are .
A forgotten and untouched passage,
  beneath the desert stars.

Photo by Mike Twardoski

A Touch of Color

It's been quite a while since I've ridden for miles.
  It's been a long, long time.
It's been quite a spell, I'm here to tell,
  since I've seen what I've held in my mind.

So give me a fire and before I retire,
  tell me a long tall tale.
Tell me your lies until I close my eyes
  and sleep slowly prevails.

Tell me the time of those buckin' horse rides
  when you won all the go 'rounds.
When that horse changed his course,
  threw you high in the air and both feet landed flat on the ground.

Just tell me a story with all of its glory.
  It's been so long I've forgotten them all.
Don't change a word or a single darn verb,
  tell 'em long, tell 'em wrong, tell 'em tall.

The cowboys these days seldom do sway
  from the truth of the story ya see.
They seldom do wander from the thoughts they do ponder.
  It's truly a mystery to me.

I like a feller that adds a "Touch of Color"
 to the long tall tales he tells.
So if there's a whopper you may have to offer,
 it would make me happy as hell.

I must confess that a little BS,
 fills in what life just don't happen to be.
It's folks just like you that takes what's not true
 and turns 'em into reality.

So tell me a story in all of its glory
 and stretch it as far as she'll go.
I'll sit and listen, not a word I'll be missin'.
 Tell me something that just ain't so.

You may go to hell for the stories you tell,
 but I'm sure there will be quite a crowd.
We'll be waitin' for you to tell stories not true.
 Tell 'em long, tell 'em wrong, tell 'em proud.

There's only one thing that I ask as the future does pass.
 Could ya do a small favor for me?
If I may be included in the tales you've polluted,
 make me a small bit of history.

Make my ol' hat not so wore out and flat
 and my ol' horse not so ugly and bare.
Make me a bit taller, make the girls do faller
 And, for Pete's sake, give me some hair.

See that old truck of mine, make it with a hard waxed shine,
  and that trailer make 'er brand new.
As you're confessin', could ya make my profession
  something most folks would like to pursue.

My ol' life is boring, so before I am snoring
  fill my head with a couple a lies.
Tell me a dandy, coat it with sugar and candy.
  Tell me something to spruce up my life.

So give me a fire and before I retire,
  tell me a story, my friend.
Tell me your lies until I close my eyes
  and this day finally comes to an end.

Ike Mathers

The mornin' sun rose, the sky was clear,
   the mountain flowers covered the ground.
A small herd of elk busted up the steep hill.
   A bull made a curious sound.

I wound down the trail, starin' down at the basin.
   It was a site that very few see.
Rock slides, cliffs, long mountain meadows,
   a breeze swayin' lone weathered trees.

About a day's ride to the lake for some fishin',
   haven't been there for thirty some years.
My heart is hopin' that the fishin' is as good,
   as good as when I was a kid.

The mornin' sun turns to an afternoon blaze,
   the sweat builds under my hat.
With the mountains so pretty and the weather so clear,
   I'm happy right here where I'm at.

As I crest over the top, the lake comes in sight,
   it takes me way back in time.
Nothin' has changed, the lake looks the same.
   I think my stay will work out just fine.

The cabin is old, but she's still standin'.
    Now the trees are a bit taller these days.
The shelves are still stocked from the Cowboys that use her.
    The old stove has somethin' to say.

The sun settles down behind the ridge tops,
    the breeze feels good off the lake.
I cook up some grub, settle down for a meal,
    this evenin's not too hard to take.

The evenin' weighs heavy on these ol' eyes of mine,
    just about to pack her in.
A noise from outside brings me up from the bunk,
    at first I thought it was wind.

Pulled the door open and to my surprise,
    stood an ol' man with a mule just as gray.
He smiled, said "Howdy", I invited him in,
    asked if he'd like to stay.

He took up my offer and found him a spot.
    He looked tired and at his wits end.
His age kind of shook me, bein' out all alone,
    said. "How ya fairin' my friend?"

He gave me a chuckle and looked me straight in the eyes,
    said "I'm doin' just fine.
You don't remember just who I am, Kid.
    It's been a long, long time."

I stared and I looked and it finally hit me,
    said "Ike, it just can't be you."
He giggled and spit,
    Said, "You're a bit older but I guess that I am, too."

We talked about times from way back when,
    about my ol' man and when I was a kid.
I told him "He passed, several years back.
    It sure was a good life he lived."

I asked how old he was these days.
    He told me, "Don't give it no mind."
We talked and talked most of the night,
    a place way back in time.

The next morning I cooked up a good Cowboy's breakfast.
    He ate it like he was a kid.
He packed up his mule, I shook his ol' hand,
    and asked, "Ike, how do you live?"

He smiled and said, "I liked to wander
    over these mountain you see.
The winter might get me one of these days,
    but that's just the way it should be."

He rode out of sight, I stood and stared,
    but I know it's the best way for him.
I enjoyed our short visit, relivin' our past,
    I enjoyed my ol' long lost friend.

I stayed a few days and then headed on out,
    really not wantin' to go.
Wound my way out to my truck and my trailer
    and slowly made it back home.

A month had gone by and a buddy stopped in.
    Hadn't seen him for quite a spell.
I said, "You won't believe what I'm about to tell ya.
    I've got a strange story to tell."

I told him of Ike and the evenin' we shared
    back in the mountains that night.
He looked at the ground, looked real profound,
    then he looked me straight in the eyes.

He said, "I don't know how to tell ya,
    and don't know what happened up there.
But I do know one thing about ol' Ike Mathers,
    he's been dead for twenty-some years."

Warm Side

The frost scatters cross the mountain trail.
    The air is brisk and clean.
The sun is peaking over the hills.
    There's ice formed across the stream.

The sun is slowly comin' ,
    the deep blue sky it fills.
We slowly meander and make our way
    to the warm side of the hill.

The winter sky is lovely,
    but she has a little bite.
Her teeth are a tad bit sharper
    in the middle of the night.

But I wouldn't trade a single day,
    not for all the wealth around.
Ya know life is sure worth livin'
    when frost is scattered 'cross the ground.

The canyons are as deep
    as the colors they display.
The greens, blues and the weathered trees
    fill the valley as we make our way.

You know the warmth the sun will give,
    how good that it will feel.
When we slowly meander and make our way
    to the warm side of the hill.

You think the horses don't give a care
   if they are cold or warm.
I'd guess I'd have to differ with you,
   might say that you were wrong.

Their tails swag as the sun does shine,
   their ears they stand up right.
They act a little different
   when the sun goes out of sight.

So if I die just take my hide
   where the world is oh, surreal.
I hope you'll lay my body down
   on the warm side of the hill.

When the sun is warm
   I sit to take in a mountain scene.
As the day does past, I lay in the grass,
   pursue a mid-day dream.

When it's been too long I feel a dog
   standing over me.
It's time to ride across the mountainside,
   back to reality.

Make my way as the sun fades away,
   the day turns cold once more.
Build a fire and wonder
   what the night may have in store.

The Gathering

When the chill fills up the evening
   there's nothing much better then a good warm meal.
Except when you meander and make your way
   to the warm side of the hill.

So if life is gettin' to ya,
   your cup is over filled,
Just take a little journey,
   to the warm side of the hill.

Photo by Lauri Gallion

Shorty

I know this cowboy who just lives down the road.
    He's a character I'm here to say.

He ain't all that tall, maybe five-foot-two.
    He walks with a bit of sway.

Him and his wife put up with each other.
    By bedtime the air would turn cold.

She got fed up with the life she had been livin'.
    She left that ornery old soul.

It wasn't too long until she found her another.
    It wasn't a real big surprise.

But when Shorty found out that it was his brother,
    you should have seen the look in his eyes.

Now brothers are brothers and blood is blood.
    Not a word was mentioned of it.

They helped out each other just like before,
    'though it hurt ol' Shorty a bit.

When their father had died several years later,
    it was his tractor that he willed to him.

Ol' Shorty took pride knowing it was his father's,
    to Shorty it was worth more the gems.

The Gathering

One summer's day his brother came by,
   had some haying he needed to do.

He looked at the ground and finally approached him.
   It was Shorty's tractor the brother pursued.

Now the tractor was all that Shorty had left
   since his marriage had gone gunnysack.

Shorty cocked his left eye then pushed his hat up high,
   said "For Pete's sake, I want this one back."

Photo by Michael Whitaker

77

Life On An Ol' Ranch

D   G   D
Saddles, bridles and dust driven days.
D   A
A house from the thirties, a child on the way.
D   G   D
Hawked right to heaven, the banker can't see.
D   A   D
The life a of a rancher is just meant to be.

D   G   D
Roundin' up the cattle, life on the land.
D   A
Tired and wore out, he's a hard-driven man.
D   G   D
But it's a good feelin' when the suns settin' down.
D   A   D
A small ranch in nowhere about ten miles from town.

G   D
It's the life of a rancher, a life on their own.
D   A
This run down ol' ranch is a place they call home.
G   A   D   G
Raisin' the children in a place that few know.
D   A   D
Life on an ol' ranch where time moves so slow.

Three generations have covered this land.
His gran'dad did pass on the Circle-Bar brand.
Wagons of years past now sit in the barn.
Covered in dust, protected from harm.

His mom and father have moved into town,
Too old for ranchin', but they still get around.
Emptiness fills his ol' father's eyes.
He misses the cattle, the herdin' and cries.

It was the life of a rancher, a life on their own.
This run-down ol' ranch was a place they called home.
Raised all their children in a place that few know.
Life on an ol' ranch where time moves so slow.

The prices are down, there's no rain in sight.
They did their damnedest, one hell of a fight.
Progress is healthy, these folks disagree.
The life a of a rancher is just meant to be.

Ninety-some years this ranch held its ground.
Times run against 'em, they'll be shuttin' 'er down.
They'll sell off the cattle, the house will be gone,
But the ways of the cowboys will still linger on.

It was the life of a rancher, a life on their own.
This run-down ol' ranch was a place they called home.
Raisin' the children in a place that few know.
Life on an ol' ranch where time moves so slow.

Life on an ol' ranch just where did it go?

Music and Lyrics by Michael Whitaker

Without Sayin'

Throws a log on the fire, he's cold and he's tired.
　　The rain pounds against the tent.
Puts on the pot, the fire sizzlin' hot.
　　Waitin' for the day to commence.

His pard wakes up and he hands him a cup,
　　his eyes half-open, half-blurred.
It's not a good day to be a Cowboy.
　　They go on without sayin' a word.

Pull out the slickers, their horses now nicker,
　　then down the trail they make their way.
Headin' for a ranch, hopin' for a chance
　　of drawin' not enough pay.

The sky's full of lightenin', the horses are frightened,
　　through the brush runs an elk herd.
It's not a good day to be a Cowboy.
　　They go on without sayin' a word.

Head over the top of this land that's forgot
　　and head down the other side.
Make their way through the mountains,
　　these cowboys were countin' on weather to be half dry.

But the wind starts to blow, it's loaded with snow,
　　somehow they thought it was spring.
It's not a good day to be a Cowboy.
　　They go on without sayin' a thing.

Make their way 'cross the river, they both shake and shiver,
    find a spot and hold up for the night.
Rig up the tent, tired and half bent,
    now the fire is feelin' just right.

Cook up some grub, a cup of hot steamin' mud,
    the meal is a little bit burnt.
It's not a good day to be a Cowboy.
    They go on without sayin' a word.

The night settles down, their bedrolls are found,
    and they sleep like a couple of pups.
When they wake in the morning, the sun is now showin'.
    It's not too hard for them to get up.

The ol' sky is blue, the sun's shinin' through
    and life looks a bit like spring.
It's a good day to be a Cowboy.
    They smile without sayin' a thing.

The flatlands they're headed, from the mountains they've dreaded,
    now comin' upon a cow town.
A hot bath is waitin', both anticipatin'
    that saloon that soon will be found.

Both a little bit frisky, they order up whiskey,
    meet some ladies not wearin' rings.
It's a good day to be a Cowboy.
    They smile without sayin' a thing.

The next day they head out, across the desert's their route,
    then they head on up to ol' Cheyenne.
Bankin' on chance, they head to the ranch,
    to see if they are hirin' hands.

That ornery ol' ranch boss points out to the bunk house,
    seems the cowboys have found them a stay.
It's a good day to be a Cowboy.
    They smile without nothin' to say.

Through all our attrition, this cowboy tradition
    is faded into a dream.
I can still see those two ol' Cowboys
    runnin' cattle through a slow movin' stream.

The Ride

This ol' boy looks like a train wreck,
    he's rode too many miles.
A life that's hard as granite,
    he still musters up a smile.

You can tell he doesn't need no help,
    he gets it on his own.
Lost a few years of livin',
    all the oats this ol' boy's sown.

I wonder what his hat would say
    if it could only talk.
I wonder what his boots could tell
    from all the miles they've walked.

The ol' pick-up that he's drivin'
    might have a thing or two to say.
That horse trailer that he's draggin'
    has seen its better days.

Someone should write a book
    about all the things he's done.
From the late nights at the local bars
    down to the settin' suns.

But I wonder if he ever thinks
    about the things he may have missed.
Like a home out in the country,
    a wife and all the kids.

They say he was the very best,
    rode the bulls with grace.
They say he would have lasted,
    but didn't know how to pace.

He'd climb upon those twisters,
    would give a nod to let 'em go.
You could never tell the pain he felt.
    It was somethin' that didn't show.

The young bull riders have heard of his name,
    but will never understand
What it takes to ride bulls, like him
    It takes a certain kind of man.

He lives like there's no tomorrow.
    You know, it may be true.
With a junkyard for a body,
    there just ain't much that he can do.

He still has all the memories,
    the buckles that he's won.
Those ol' boots of his still fit just fine,
    that truck of his still runs.

The money and the glory,
    somehow has slipped away.
But if that ol' hat of his could only talk
    I'd like hear what it would say.

Old Boys

I wish I was an old man
   that had gone a mile or two.
Back in the old days
   when life was straight and true.

When the fish they caught were two pounds
   and the deer had horns galore.
I wish I could have lived back then
   to watch the eagles soar.

A pack string a quarter mile long,
   the mules, the best that could be found.
You cut your way into hills
   and not another soul around.

The canvases that laid across the mules,
   were used as flies at night.
The sky so clear you could feel the moon.
   I bet that was a sight.

The cabins scattered across the hills,
   were used by one and all.
The trees that lined the hillsides,
   were standing green and tall.

Ya see I wish I was an old man,
   the kind that held his own.
Back about a hundred years,
   out on the trail alone.

When a sack of flour and some fixin's
	was all a man would need.
The meat came from the hills around
	and the water from the streams.

When a tent beam came from a tree branch
	and the rope came from a pack.
When a cup of coffee was filled with grounds,
	a little thick and way too black.

When all you had were stories
	to fill the time of day.
I wish I was an old man
	and had lived my life that way.

Most don't understand me
	and the life I somehow missed.
Born a hundred years too late.
	it will have to stay a wish.

But I could just imagine,
	the life these old boys led.
Stars shining right above them
	on the ground they made their beds.

Now when I travel down the trails
	I follow fancy signs.
I'm sure that these old cowboys
	searched for blazes in the pines.

A rock would be their marker,
　　a creek would lead their way.
I wish I was a cowboy,
　　back in the packin' days.

But all I have are the hills
　　they traveled once before.
I can't help but think about them,
　　when I see an eagle soar.

Now I wish I was an old man
　　that had gone a mile or two.
A pack string a quarter mile long,
　　a time I wish I knew.

Mountain Rodeo

The day started out just like all the rest.
  The sky was clear and blue.
But what was comin' at me
  is somethin' I wish I never knew.

I should have just laid there
  in that warm old sack of mine.
Should have enjoyed this purty mornin'
  the kind you rarely find.

Headin' out from a long old ride,
  hated to see it end.
But I had some obligations,
  needed to meet up with a friend.

We just had made it to the top,
  was headin' down the other side.
When I met up with a problem,
  the kind where ya almost died.

Sittin' in my saddle,
  a stock of grass hangin' from my mouth.
The mule that was a trailin'
  turned around and headed south.

Searchin' for the problem,
  I quickly turned to see.
Then it hit me right between the eyes,
  there was a swarm of buzzin' bees.

The Gathering

Been to the big ol' Rodeos,
    seen a display of skill and guts.
At times I think those cowboys
    are plumb crazy, even nuts.

But at this very moment
    they can't hold a candle to dear ol' me.
See, they don't have to ride those big ol' bulls,
    through the timber swattin' bees.

Off the side we headed.
    Now I was the one in tow.
Where we would finally end up,
    the good lord would surely know.

Somehow the lead went around my hand,
    and through the air I flew.
Like Superman on a real bad day,
    a tree I now pursued.

Just when I clipped a branch
    and thought I came to rest,
The slack jerked out of that lead rope,
    and you can guess the rest.

Down the side of that old mountain,
    just a skiddin' on the ground.
I reached down for my ol' pocket knife,
    but it weren't to be found.

I caught a rock right side my head.
    It knocked me right out flat.
From then on I don't remember much,
    Not sure just where I's at.

I thought I woke in heaven.
   I knew I was dead for sure.
Heaven looked real purty,
   and had the essence of manure.

But when things came to focus
   and I could finally see.
There, standin' right above me,
   was my mule starin' down at me.

My horse let out a whinny,
   it sounded like a laugh.
I stood up with my brim ripped off.
   My head had a big ol' gash.

Some regroupin' was in order,
   and we got back on that ol' trail.
Even though I was just a little sore,
   my face was mighty pale.

I mounted that ol' horse of mine,
   and we headed on a lope.
If that damn ol' mule was comin'
   he'd have to do 'er without a rope.

Now the Rodeos have bulls and broncs,
   the toughest by the rule.
The best buckin' stock in this here land,
   but I've never seen a mule.

It's Nothin'

She always gets up ahead of the rest
before the sun starts its day.

Pullin' out pans and pancake mix
makin' breakfast her own way.

Boilin' coffee, sausage fryin' in the pan,
the clank of plates dealt like cards.

The cowboys do gripe about their hard-driven lives.
To her it doesn't seem all that hard.

By the time they all rise the wood stove is hot.
The room smells as good as it gets.

The table is full of a breakfast for kings.
Her life isn't full of regrets.

By the time they had finished their lunches are made,
Their clothes are all stacked neat into piles.

They complain and moan of the life they have known.
She stands at the sink and just smiles.

Off on their horses the cowboys do ride.
The kitchen is a sight to see.

The Gathering

She grabs her dish tub, loads up the sink,
starts to scrub' til the plates are clean.

Then comes a beller from out by the barn.
She heads out to see what is wrong.

The ol' cow is calvin' and havin' a time,
seems things are takin' too long.

She reaches down to help out,
finds a couple of legs, pulls with all of her might.

Here comes the calf, the cow settles down,
seems everything works out just right.

Goes in the barn and feeds while she's there,
then grabs an armload of wood.

Goes back in the house to finish her chores,
to a life that is understood.

The morning does warm, the ranch shows its charm,
then to the store in a truck that's half bent.

Pulls down the long drive, she pulls off to the side,
to mend a broken down fence.

Started cookin' supper up early,
then folds clothes from off of the line.

One of the cowboys is havin' a birthday,
bakes a cake in her spare time.

Now darkness is sneakin' and the air cools down.
The cowboys ride into sight.

Supper is waitin', the wood stove is hot.
The day now turns into night.

They eat up their meals, she brings in the cake.
They sing to their dear old friend.

The cowboys retire one after another.
She cleans up the mess once again.

The ranch is now quiet, she has some time to herself.
By the fire she has some readin' to do.

Her eyes start to close her chin drops to her chest,
seems her day is finally through.

She staggers to bed, lays down her head,
sets her alarm for another day.

But she's thankful that she's not a cowboy,
it would be hard livin' life that way.

One Day Too Many

The evenings are long. It's cold in the mornings.
    The sun shines, but the warmth isn't there.
The ponds are all frozen. The geese have flown south.
    The horses have shaggy long hair.

He chops some more wood even though he's got plenty,
    heads to the kitchen to see what is there.
Warms up some coffee, sits next to the fire,
    reads a letter from a daughter who cares.

Stumbles the long afternoon away.
    Reads a book 'til the sun goes down.
Cooks him some supper even though he's not hungry.
    The ol' place shows no trace of sound.

The life he once shared with a woman so fair
    is the life he still wishes he had.
Now he lives all alone in this place he calls home,
    pretendin' it's not all that bad.

He fixes pack boxes even though they are fine,
    then he yawns and he heads off to bed.
Turns off the lantern, he pulls up the covers,
    grabs a pillow and lays down his head.

He dreams of the times when his wife was still there.
    Livin' too long is a crime.
He's fit as a fiddle; his spirit has left him,
    livin' life at seventy-nine.

The evenings are long and it's cold in the mornings.
    Spring is a long ways away.
He tends to his horses. It's all he has left,
    an old man with too many days.

A Forgotten Past

The mothers of tradition
   have faced the course of time.
The forgotten hardships they endured,
   the wearing and the grind.

These women from a time long past,
   they soon have been forgot.
The sacrifices that they all made,
   the dreams that they all sought.

The keeping it together,
   the mending of the clothes,
The sickened child, the many miles,
   the long and hardened road.

The scorch of the summer sun,
   the bite of winter nights.
They lay now in history,
   few words written of their lives.

The history books have written
   of the men of honored fame.
The strength that they've shown,
   the mountains they have tamed.

But history has forgotten
   a few heroes of yesterday.
Their lives they surely gave us
   in each and every way.

The tending of the family
    while their husbands did explore.
The fixing of the wagons,
    the tending to a sore.

The fever of the husbands,
    the laying them to rest.
Proceeding on their very own
    to tame the rugged west.

In modern days of farming
    her presence stands again.
The tending of the cattle,
    the fence that she must mend.

The raising of the children,
    the books that she must keep.
The unrelenting chores she knows
    after her family's fast asleep.

The quiet presence she has shown
    through recorded history,
In some ways unforgivable,
    a sadden tragedy.

Women in the chase of dreams
    many years ago.
A time history has forgotten,
    a time that few now know.

The Gathering

A beat and tattered wagon
    pulled by a withered ox.
Women of the great expansion,
    a time that history has forgot.

So, change the course of history
    and how it may be told.
Learn from what these women have given us.
    so many years ago.

Photo by Bill Gallion

Lauri Gallion and her pack string.

The Ghost

I've told this story but to very few.
　　It took place back a year or two.
I was walkin' through this ghost town that died,
　　old buildin's that were old and dried.

The windows there were mostly gone,
　　the doors were hangin', but not for long.
The floors they barely held my feet,
　　but this one saloon was still nice and neat.

The shelves were lined with booze and all.
　　The glasses all stood clean and tall.
The piano keys were free from dust.
　　The spittoon didn't show no signs of rust.

Then the strangest thing happened, you see,
　　I asked for a drink and someone answered me.
There wasn't a soul for a hundred miles.
　　I could not move, I just stood and smiled.

Not knowin' if my mind played a trick on me,
　　I asked the bartender that I couldn't see
If he could pour me a glass of sour mash.
　　He answered "Yep" and I then ran real fast.

The Gathering

I slipped down the street of that ol' ghost town,
    not knowing what I had really found.
Then I heard a shot that was meant to kill.
    Then a voice yelled out, "You didn't pay your bill!"

I stopped right there, dead in my tracks,
    I slowly turned and headed back.
Went in that bar and to my surprise,
    there stood that ghost before my eyes.

He said, "I really didn't mean to throw a scare,
    but the drink you ordered is sittin' there."
I hate to see mash go to waste,
    so I grabbed that glass and took a taste.

At a time like this it tasted good,
    even though this couldn't be understood.
We sat and talked the time away.
    He told me about the ol' Cowboy days.

I drank until I couldn't drink no more,
    fell off my stool onto the floor.
Must have laid there until the break of dawn.
    When I woke the ghost was dead and gone.

The bar was old and covered with dust,
    the spittoon I saw was filled with rust.
The glasses were broke upon that shelf,
    I yelled but I was by myself.

I looked at that bottle lying next to me,
    it read "Wild Turkey 1993."
I hadn't seen a ghost at all.
    The only spirit I saw went down my craw.

So I walked out of that deserted town.
    It wasn't a ghost that I had found.
I heard a shot that was meant to kill,
    then a voice yelled out,
"Are you going to pay your bill?"

The Crossing

A pack string eight mules deep
   headin' down the grade.
The sun, she was a shinin',
   the snow laid high within the shade.

The river came into view,
   the bridge was around the slide.
Then a feelin' came over him,
   a feelin' he couldn't hide.

When he rounded the painted cliffs,
   he looked upon that long span bridge.
There was a Cowboy that he knew so well,
   with a young pony that would not give.

He went to help that Cowboy,
   but that young horse was way too scared.
On the bridge, the string was hung up.
   He knew that time would wear.

Then a thought came across his mind.
   He had thoughts of years ago.
When his gran'dad made this crossing
   there was no bridge to toll.

Years ago they crossed the rapids
   right where this bridge does lie.
He knew if gran'dad were here today
   he'd hit here fast and high.

Then an urge came across that Cowboy.
   Down the rocky banks they went.
His mules trailin' right behind
   on that steep rockslide decent.

They hit the water at full speed,
   the white water moving fast.
The horse he rode was a sire,
   from his grandpa's breed of past.

The nose of his trusty steed
   was flared with shades of red.
He knew if he were to make it,
   he'd have to give that horse his head.

The mules dug in with packs afloat,
   the river pushed 'em down.
He yelled with all his spirit.
   He had thoughts that they would drown.

The string stretched down that river.
   The ropes were stretchin' thin.
Another yell ran through the air.
   There was no givin' in.

Then land was at his horse's hooves,
   up the steep hillside they went.
Digging through that shale bank,
   mules claiming the ascent.

Then flat ground laid beneath their feet.
   He gave the string a rest.
His chest was loudly pounding,
   he knew they did their best.

He looked upon that ol' Cowboy,
   his face was covered with a grin.
That ol' Cowboy smiled with weathered eyes
   and tipped his hat to him.

That young Cowboy stood with pride.
   He understood just what he'd done.
For that Ol' Cowboy standin' on that bridge
   was his ol' grandfather's son.

The Right Decision

Now every man has crossroads.
  You know the decision he must make.

Sometimes it's hard to handle,
  a bit more than he can take.

So here I sit upon my horse,
  dumb-founded and confused.

A decision way too big for me,
  I guess I'll have to choose.

Now I've been to every place I see
  that's wrote upon this sign.

I think it'll get the best of me,
  I may just lose my mind.

Oh, Fish Lake is just up the trail.
  It's not that far, ya see.

But in the spring ol' Dumbbell
  is as purty as can be.

North, South, East or West,
  I just can not decide.

Sometimes things get confusin'
  when you're on a mountain ride.

They think the world leaders
  have big decisions they must make.

But, I've never seen 'em standin' here
   Pickin' out a mountain lake.

I sit here with conviction,
   strong and full of might.

My decision now has been made.
   I think I'll head her to the right.

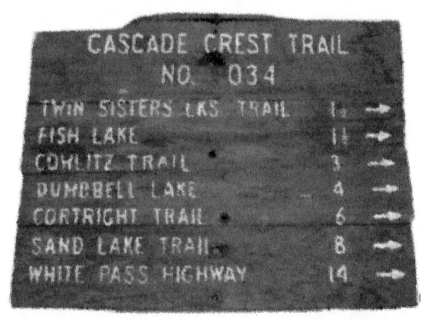

Photo by Michael Whitaker

So I take a look at this here sign,
   my wisdom's hard to hide.

I'm proud of my convictions,
   not a man to compromise.

Summer Rain

Unpacked, now the fire is burnin'.
   The wind comes off the lake.
The horses now are grazing',
   dig through the pack boxes to find the steaks.

Dig out the pots and fryin' pan,
   pull my knife to peel the spuds.
The coals are almost ready.
   The clouds they're movin' up above.

The wind kicks hard against the trees,
   I look up towards the sky.
The air turns cold and heavy.
   The steaks must wait to fry.

The drops slowly fall against the ground,
   we calmly sit and wait.
We gather and put the gear away,
   the food and our plates.

Head into the shelter,
   now the rain is pourin' down.
The fire slowly steams and fades away,
   the water runs 'cross the ground.

We lay back on our bedrolls,
   watch 'er as she pours.
Times like this used to make me mad.
   It ain't a bother anymore.

The Gathering

The rain socks in for the long haul.
    It might be here to stay.
Find some crackers and sardines,
    a good meal on a rainy day.

My ol' buddy cuts a tale or two,
    he swears that they are true.
I laugh at him, he gives a grin.
    One more story he pursues.

The weather holds on through the night,
    the drizzle helps me sleep.
In the morning we crawl from our ol' sacks,
    I slip my boots upon my feet.

The birds fill the mornin' air.
    The mornin' sky is blue.
Cook up some breakfast on an open fire;
    some steak and eggs will do.

Head out for some fishin'.
    The horse's heads are down.
Scan the hills for goats and elk,
    just to see if they're around.

An open mind is helpful
    when the rain does come your way.
Plans sometimes do take a change
    when you're on a mountain stay.

The creeks they are a flowin'.
    The ground she slowly dries.
The day is down right purty
    with that sun up in the sky.

Nothin's hurt and there's nothin' lost.
    It's just a simple fact of life.
Life don't get much better,
    when the rain pours through the night.

The Lost Trail

His journey took him to long ago,
    a trail full of times gone by.
A ribbon of dirt that runs on forever
    under the open sky.

A sorrel horse, a long eared mule,
    supplies to last a week.
A snubbed-nose dog just up ahead.
    Old times this cowboy seeks.

The landscape hadn't change a bit,
    the creek runs pure and clear.
The trail's now a bit over grown.
    It's been nearly thirty years.

He has an eye of happiness,
    a smile across his face.
He kicks his sorrel in the ribs,
    stiffens up the pace.

He made it to the very crest,
    halfway into his trip.
He sits and stares for a hundred miles,
    from his jug he takes a sip.

A back country celebration,
    a life that he once lived.
A simple understandin',
    of what this land can give.

The days now pass one by one.
   This trail is hard to find.
It felt somewhat unfamiliar.
   It started weighing on his mind.

There came a point of closure,
   somehow he felt he failed.
See, there would be no tomorrow,
   you can't ride an old lost trail.

The countryside's too rugged,
   he couldn't get around.
The sun was surely fading.
   He decided to settle down.

He knew that it was over,
   no one uses her no more.
He knew it was now history,
   a tale from long before.

He realized that this old trail
   isn't used by folks these days.
He realized an ending,
   nature now has got her way.

He now is on a short list
   of a long-lost dying breed.
There's very few from a life he knew.
   No one now feels the need.

The Gathering

He settled for the night ahead
　　on a trail from long ago.
Underneath the lanterns in the sky,
　　a life this cowboy knows.

He turned back in the morning.
　　He shook his head in disbelief.
He ponders times from way back when,
　　old memories that he keeps.

A sorrel and a long eared mule,
　　a simple cowboy's tale.
A snubbed-nose dog just up ahead,
　　running down an old lost trail.

A Gathering Storm

His long day has ended, the fences are mended,
    and the ranch house is a long way away.
The wind sieves through the trees, burnt grass sways
    in the breeze, the low sun is closing the day.

The cool air he's feeling, the moon soon will be stealing
    the light that paves his way home.
The clouds make their way at the close of this day.
    There's a sense of a gathering storm.

Cuts through the hollow, the creek he now follows
    towards a shelter that waits ahead.
The air turns to a shiver as he crosses the river
    from where the lower valley is fed.

The sun heads into hiding, the horse he is riding
    steps it up as they make their way home.
He turns up his collar, the sun's getting smaller.
    He can see the gathering storm.

The clouds roll over the hills, the sky overfills
    with colors of black and gray.
The tree branches bend, it's a message they send
    that they best get on their way.

The lightening does build, then it cuts loose at will,
    just a horse and a cowboy alone.
They look straight ahead, they have no time to dread
    the might of the gathering storm.

The Gathering

As they trot through the field, it's a hard rain they feel.
  The barn now comes into sight.
The rain pours down, the sky's filled with sounds
  on this cold and windy night.

The lights start to show, 'cross the flatlands they glow,
  and they stand out so all alone.
He rides in the barn from the presence of harm,
  as he eyes the gathering storm.

Puts his pony away, feeds him some hay
  as the thunder rattles the roof.
His old horse is frightened from the thunder and lightenin'.
  His horse casts sounds of chattering hoofs.

He talks to him gentle, gets him to settle.
  He settles to a weary calm.
As he heads on inside, he looks towards the sky,
  and watches the gathering storm.

Builds him a fire, he's wore-out and tired,
  takes a sip of blended whiskey.
The fire from the stove, warms his body and soul,
  he now has a reason to be .

Things now are right, as he settles down for the night,
  he enjoys the comforts of home.
Through the window he stares at the cold dark air,
  and enjoys the gathering storm.

It's a day, oh, so common of this land he's grown up on.
   It's a life he lives on his own.
Some say it's his way; he enjoys stormy days.
   Some say it's all that he's known.

It's a lesson of life, the pain and the strife,
   it's a peace that he finds at home.
It's the fire that glows, how it fills up his soul
   in the midst of a gathering storm.

Johnson Creek

I looked towards the sky and things didn't look good,
But Rod was ready to go.
Our knowledge of planes and the basics of flight
Was somethin' that just didn't show.

But he lifted her up with nothin' to see
But fog and a spot here and there.
Our trust in ol' Rod was as solid as steel,
And we left without a care.

It wasn't too long 'til things seemed to go wrong.
See, the fog started rollin' in.
Hills to the left, hills to the right.
At this point Paul lost his grin.

Rod's eyes danced from side to side,
But he seemed so calm and cool.
He circled and searched, just lookin' for a hole
And decidin' if we were fools.

The fog dropped down as we rounded this town,
"Yellow Pine," Rod whispered to me.
He banked hard left and down quickly we went,
Then we landed at Johnson Creek.

Once on the ground the Sheriff came along,
Said, "Bonnie's been lookin' for you."
Rod borrowed his phone, told her where we had flown
And that everything was cool.

Then the two pilots huddled, their voices were muddled,
And the final decision was made.
They fired 'em up and again we took off,
We knew we had it made in the shade.

But things were still soupy and ol' Paul was more droopy.
See, the fog had us completely surrounded,
But ol' Rod was not shaken, not a second thought taken,
Hell, that when my heart started poundin'.

He circled 'er higher and to my surprise,
A small hole in the fog soon appeared.
You know, I ponder about these small plane trips
We seem to take year after year.

I guess where I'm goin' with this long drawn out tale
Is a horse maybe a better way to go?
But I know that next year we'll be sittin' right here,
Next to Rod in the fog and the snow.

Photo by Michael Whitaker

To Rod and the Gang at McCall Air Taxi

Back Yonder

The twilight was sneakin' up over the ridge,
   the stars were fadin' away.
The rustle of pans, the shimmerin' fire,
   meant the day was well on its way.

One after another the Cowboys woke up,
   stumbled their way to the fire.
Grabbin' a cup of ol' Cooky's coffee,
   their bones were cold and tired.

Just a day's ride 'til home would be found;
   a shelter, a good warm bed,
A cast iron stove, a good solid meal,
   a soft place to lay their heads.

Their clothes were filthy, a wash pan was needed.
   Their hands were black as the night.
The horses now strolled, just a bit tired,
   they rode on in the mornin' light.

Headin' on home from a long cattle drive,
   at best it was a long steady grind.
The country now looks a bit more familiar,
   to most this was a good sign.

Now the Cowboys of old were rugged and bold,
   the lives they lived were hard.
Ridin' the plains, eating dust all the way,
   the cold nights under the stars.

In the days of the drives, in the ol' Cowboy's lives,
    an unspoken peace could be found.
Just ridin' their horses on meanderin' courses,
    pushin' cattle 'cross the ol' desert ground.

Back in the day, they liked it this way.
    Most had nowhere to go.
It got in their blood, the dust, the mud,
    the hot sun and the cold winter snow.

The calvin', the brandin', the tendin' of cattle,
    the one more horse that needs broke.
The bendin', the mendin', repairin' the saddles;
    not a regret would ever be spoke.

A job was a job, pay was still pay,
    a life that they came to know.
An ol' Cowboy's tale, where hard work prevails,
    sometimes taking its toll.

The railroad grew closer, time soon would change.
    Most weren't needed no more.
The cattle drives died, the cold starry nights,
    the tendin,' the mendin', the chores.

The old cowboy ways, soon faded away.
    The age of the engine was here;
The whistles, the steam, the new western dream.
    It was something the cowboys feared.

Now the herds were loaded on the new cattle cars,
    they bellered as the train whistle blew.
The ride to the ranch just wasn't that far;
    not as far as a time they once knew.

I can't help but ponder of that time way back yonder,
    when the ways of the cowboy prevailed.
Seems somewhere out there in the hot desert air,
    still lingers an ol' Cowboy's tale.

Two Ol' Boys

Two ol' boys a ridin'
  along a windin' river trail.
The sky turns mean with thunder,
  it opens up with hail.

The storm does kick up a bit,
  the wind is strong and cool.
Two ol' boys a ridin'
  a couple horses with a mule.

The storm slowly passes by,
  like a thief within the night.
The sky opens up a bit,
  the sun slowly comes in sight.

A song that they've heard before,
  a life they've come to know.
Two ol' boys a ridin'
  along a river running cold.

But they don't seem to mind it.
  It's all these two have known.
A couple of crusty Cowboys,
  ridin' canyons all alone.

Not much for conversation,
  they just stare at the hills above.
A country that takes your breath away,
  a country they do love.

The ranch lays just round the bend
    where herdin' jobs await.
The tough ol' lives that they bear
    are based on luck or maybe fate.

The ranchers always hire them,
    together they're a tool.
When other Cowboys dog them,
    they send them back to school.

They work together with every motion,
    not a word is ever said.
Just two ol' boys a ridin',
    together 'til they're dead.

They usually keep to themselves;
    don't have a lot to say.
They sit and listen to the Cowboys
    at the ending of the day.

When the cattle's sold off
    they draw their final pay.
Not a word is ever spoken.
    They just up and ride away.

Two ol' ornery cusses
    that live their lives alone.
Two horses with a long eared mule,
    their saddles are their home.

The Cowboys scratch their heads,
    give these boys a sneer.
But like the tickin' of a clock,
    they'll be back again next year.

Don't know where they are headed,
    don't care where they've been.
Just two ol' boys a ridin'
    on a winding trail again.

Peckin' Order

Roamin' 'cross the lower plains, lookin' for some work
I ran across a cattle ranch that was gatherin' up its herd.

I knew that this could only mean that a cattle drive was near.
See, they head them down the dusty trail at the end of every year.

So, I said to this here cowboy, "Ya know if they're hirin' hands?"
He said, "We're short a few, but it's best to ask the man."

But when I ask just where he was, the cowboy gave a grin.
He laughed and said, "Don't never mind, you best just join on in."

Well it took a while to figure out, who the boss was of this show.
At least a couple goldarn weeks, for a hand like me to know.

I thought it could be big Bob Ketchum, the way he stood so proud.
When I asked one of the other hands, he said, "For cryin' out loud."

Then Dusty Wilson came to mind, he's the oldest cowboy here.
But when the cattle drive did start, he quietly took the rear.

Butch McCoy could be the boy, 'cause he sits in his saddle tall.
By the way the cowboys bark at him, knew it wasn't him at all.

Then Curly Stone kept all alone, I guess he'd be my choice.
But I hear he hasn't talked in years, see, he somehow lost his voice.

I hope it's not that Little Pete, it would be real hard to take.
See, at five foot three and two left feet it'd be a big mistake.

My guessin' it went on and on, I didn't have a clue.
Ol' Scar Face Bob, you rotten slob, I pray it just ain't you.

After days on end the chuck wagon finally joined the cattle drive.
Just about to starve to death, ham hocks and beans kept me alive.

The supper chime rang just in time and the cowboys did line up,
Standin' still and patiently with their plates and ol' tin cups.

I knew the boss was still the boss and would be the first to eat.
When cross-eyed Joe was the first to go, I nearly left my feet.

Being new I calmly waited there, the very last in line.
The smell of that corn bread, was a smell that smelled so fine.

Now this is where I came to know, who really was the boss.
Things some how got all messed up, I was standing at a loss.

See I spit a chaw across her foot, it was truly by mistake.
Starin' with those big boss eyes, she went and broke my plate.

I'd like to share some good advice, from a man that's wearin' lean.
I know you can't survive for weeks on end,
eatin' just "Ham Hocks and Beans"

Boxed Canyon

Just up this boxed canyon about twenty two miles
    is a wide spot where the creek does branch.
An open grass meadow that has life running through it,
    an honest to God working ranch.

The world has evolved into misunderstanding,
    but this ranch has stayed just the same.
Working real hard at simple traditions,
    not seeking fortune or fame.

The rancher's grandfather first started here,
    passing down tricks of the trade.
The ranch house was built back eighty some years,
    so long ago that the memories fade.

The angle does chime when it comes supper time
    and the fixin's come from years gone back.
The old barn is standin' out on her own,
    the smell lingers of old leather tack.

Tradition runs deep in the life they do keep,
    ranchin' is all that they know.
Herdin' the cattle from off the high country,
    winter is startin' to show.

The mighty rock walls from this canyon that calls
    holds the traditions of life they do teach.
The teachin' that is passed down from their mothers and fathers,
    echoes in the canyons of this sacred retreat.

An old family ranch surrounded by cliffs,
    that protects the way that they live.
Just a simple existence from years long ago,
    an old ranch that progress has missed.

Desert Sand

The burnt vast land lays under my feet.
I can see for a hundred miles.
The rolling foothills covered with sage brush and cliffs,
the rocks lay in impassable piles.

The valleys were cut from rain driven creeks
that now lay burnt and dry.
The sun is so hot I can barely breathe.
The wind blows sand in my eyes.

How in the hell could folks here exist?
The answer I don't understand.
But this ranch from years back, now lays here in ruins,
half buried by hot desert sand.

I hear that this ranch was a goin' concern,
back in the days of the silver rush.
Packers supplied the miners up high.
Now she kneels in a quiet hush.

The corral posts are leanin', the house nearly gone.
The barn is flat on the ground.
But I still hear the cowboys riggin' the mules
for the journey where silver is found.

The supper chime rings and I hear "Come and get it,"
the clank of ol' tin plates.
The Cowboys sit down, faces stare at the ground,
as the cook stumbles through grace.

The fixin' are many, the steaks sizzle hot,
    potatoes, corn and baked beans.
The good meals are few, usually ham hock stew.
    Most cowboys are slender and lean.

The ol' ranch house was made of Mexican stucco,
    the roof was made of red clay.
Life was hard, chasin' that cold shiny metal,
    back in the ol' minin' days.

Now abandoned and lonely she sits by herself,
    no one gives her much mind.
The desert sand blows, coverin' this ranch of old,
    a place that's been forgotten by time.

The tombstones are many, half covered by slow drifting sand.
    The names have been long forgot.
The lives often wasted, forgotten cowboys and faces,
    all for the silver they sought.

In the wind you can hear songs of ol' yesteryear,
    that the cowboys sung way long ago.
But few now take time to listen to ol' cowboy rhymes
    that was sung from the days of old.

The suns starts to hide, behind these rugged hillsides.
    The evening starts to retire.
I can still hear those cowboys singin' ol lullabies
    around an ol' desert fire.

They Ride

```
G              D
```
He rides in as the sun goes down;
```
G              D
```
Can't find a single soul around.
```
G           D    Bm
```
Steps off and he walks inside,
```
A      Asus4         A      Asus4
```
Stomps his boots, another day's gone by.

```
G                    D
```
Empty house with the lights left on,
```
G              D
```
not a breath , not a soul around.
```
G              D     Bm
```
A note lies there for him to read;
```
A      Asus4 A      Asus4
```
takes a chair and bends a knee.
```
C                   G
```
His eyes weep like the morning dew,
```
C                      G
```
She's gone. He doesn't know what to do,
```
A      Asus4     A     Asus4    C
```
So he rides.

```
D       Bm      G         A
```
Now years ago it's was both their dream—
```
D               Bm   G       A
```
the long evening walks by a mountain stream.
```
D       Bm        G     A
```
Tired of living from week to week,
```
C                         G
```
A new way of living this young girl seeks.
```
A       Asus4    A      Asus4
```
So she rides.
```
C       G        Asus4 A
```

This time she's gone for good.
His ways were never understood.
Tired of being a Cowboy's wife,
Tired of pain, tired of strife.

Days and months have slipped away.
He stumbles through another day.
The life he loves has become a chore,
He now knows he needs something more.

She runs away like a painted horse.
A new life, a different course.

She rides

Now years ago it was both their dream—
The long evening walks by a mountain stream.
Tired of living from week to week,
A new way of living this young girl seeks.

So she rides.

Another day he just rides his rounds,
Works his way to the upper ground.
Then down below he sees a cloud of dust,
It's her in his pick-up truck.

A love that didn't slip away,
A love that is here to stay,

He rides.

Now years have passed, they live their dream—
The long walks by a mountain stream.
A summer's day riding side by side,
A love they knew they could never hide,

And they ride.

They ride.

Lyrics by Michael Whitaker
Music by Bill Whalen

The Christmas Cabin

The weather turned a little hard
   as he crossed the upper ridge.
The pace that he was travelin'
   was all his pony had to give.

Been many years since he's been this way.
   Time wasn't on his side.
Just searchin' for a cabin
   beneath a snowy sky.

The darkness of the day was near,
   his horse was cold and tired.
Then below he spotted through the trees,
   what he thought could be a fire.

He made a straight line for it
   and there before his eyes
Was that cabin that he remembered,
   lights flickerin' through the night.

He slowly walked across the porch,
   and he gently tapped the door.
The door it slowly opened.
   There stood an ol' face from years before.

Unsaddled and put his horse away,
   came in to settle down.
There sat a needed supper.
   They passed the meal around.

Then they sat there by the fireplace,
    a moment without words.
They started singing "Silent Night."
    A harmonica was heard.

Just a Cowboy Christmas,
    the only gifts they had to share
Was a Cowboy Christmas lullaby,
    A moment, oh so rare.

They sang of the Wise Men,
    the gifts they brought that night.
They sang of baby Jesus,
    the stars shining light.

Just two ol' wranglers singin',
    of a time long, long ago.
In a cabin in the mountains,
    a Christmas Night covered in snow.

In the morning they shared a cup,
    then he pulled his saddle from the rack.
Loaded up his saddle bags,
    then he crawled upon his pony's back.

The morning sun was shining,
    across a field of snow.
Just a cabin in the mountains,
    a special place these wranglers know.

As he rode away that snowy day,
  he stopped and turned around.
He said, "Merry Christmas, Brother."
  You couldn't hear a single sound.

His brother gave him a smile,
  had thoughts of years gone by.
He whispered, "Merry Christmas,"
  with a tear drop in his eye.

Photo by Michael Whitaker

Chapter 2
Idaho

Idaho

I've spent weeks at a time in the backcountry of Idaho. Most have been on the middle fork of the Salmon River and the Big Creek drainage. The first time I flew into the backcountry of Idaho I really had no idea how pretty it would be. Had no idea of the height of the mountains, the size of the rivers and creeks. I guess I should have had a clue when the name of the creek was "Big" Creek and that it just may be a little hard to cross. It said creek, though. When the map read "Cliff" Creek that too should have raised a red flag. I'll pay attention from now on.

The abundance of deer, elk, fish and other wildlife, simply amazes me. But the best part of this country has to be the hot springs. I'll tell ya right now that after a long workout going up and down these overgrown mountains, a nice soak in one of them hot springs sure goes good with an ice cold beer. Most everywhere you go it is at least fifty miles from the nearest road. With the exception of a pack string here and there, and a few other hearty souls, you usually don't run into many folks. If you get off the main trail along the river, you probably won't see anyone at all. Being the recluse that I am, it works out just fine for me.

Speaking of airplanes and runways, well, I'd guess you could call them runways. Let's settle on calling them non- level, overly short patches of rocks and grass. Well anyway, the pilots of these mountain hoppers have to be completely nuts. We have come to know a pilot from McCall Air Taxi who has been flying in and out of the mountains his entire life. You would think the odds would eventually catch up with him. I wrote a poem, "Johnson Creek" which happens to be a true story about a four-hour plane trip that we took with Rod one foggy and snowy day.

The problem was the trip should have taken about forty -five minutes. We did a lot of circlin' in the canyons over Big Creek. Yeah I said "Big Creek."

Most of the mountains top out around ten thousand feet and the rivers usually run at three thousand feet. The problem that lies in the difference in elevation usually occurs within eight to ten miles. You do the math.

Needless to say, Idaho isn't just lava rock and potato fields. It is a vast wilderness area with scenery so pretty it will simply make you take pause.

The pack strings that you find in these areas are made up of some of the finest mules that I have ever laid eyes on. It will take ya back to an era that I wish I could have been a part of. Seems the new ways of convenience just don't have a place there.

I hope that it never changes.

Nowhere

About a three-day ride to nowhere
   is a cabin from long ago.
The long and windy winters
   have slowly taken its toll.

Not sure when they built her;
   not sure why she is there.
Just a cabin that sits in nowhere,
   for about a hundred years.

The walls are lined with history,
   junk that's been left behind.
The cooking stove is something,
   about the best that you can find.

The door must weight three hundred pounds,
   and the windows need repair.
Just a cabin that sits in nowhere,
   for about a hundred years.

The roof is mostly rotten,
   but I've never seen her leak.
The chimney is made from river rock,
   that was borrowed from the creek.

The old wood floors are wore out
   from all the boots she's held.
The only full time residents
   are the field mice that dwell.

The Gathering

But I come here in November,
    when the weather starts to change.
When a fire is appreciated
    and a lantern lights the page.

Photo by Michael Whitaker

Not sure when they built her;
    not sure why she is there.
Just a cabin that sits in nowhere
    for about a hundred years.

Don't think that she is used much.
    I'm sure she's lost in time.
Only a few of us appreciate
    such a rare and simple find.

The country that surrounds her
    is heaven here on earth.
A place that sits in nowhere,
    an under-estimated worth.

I always hate to leave her,
    and I wonder why I do.
The beauty of the country
    with a winter sky so blue.

The elk and deer graze at her side,
    no fear from being harmed.
I think they are a lot like me,
    enjoying this old gal's charm.

Her solitude is timeless,
    a long forgotten way.
Just a cabin that sits in nowhere,
    on a cold November day.

Just Ponderin'

I have a list a mile long of the things I need to do.
There are a half a ton of things that should be done,
A few things I should pursue.

I'm sure regrets and what the hecks,
Will be the first things that I say.
I have no motivation on this warm and lazy day.

So I think I'll sit and ponder, think about the little things in life;
The way the moon lights up the trees
On a pretty autumn night.

Sit so still that an ol' gray squirrel eats a peanut from my hand.
Ponder about my children
And how time has quickly ran.

It's not that I'm an old man, it's just I see some gray.
But I wouldn't change a single thing,
Not one solitary day

So I think I'll sit and ponder, think about all the things I've seen;
The high trips in the mountains,
That pretty runnin' stream.

I turn and look around me and stare at the country side;
The river runnin' past me
And the sunny autumn sky.

I think of all the huntin' trips, just me and that yahoo, Paul.
I'm glad we took the time for them,
A nice way to spend the fall.

I sit here just a ponderin' and think of the reasons why.
Why the sky is so gol darn blue,
Why the clouds hang in the sky.

Why the river runs forever, even though she's wide and deep.
Why I enjoy my dear ol' friends
And the company we keep.

I remember when the snow fell, we were trapped for several days.
But it really didn't matter much,
We still enjoyed our stay.

We had a fire a blazin', the cowboys gathered round
Tellin' all their stories,
A few new friends were found.

I really should get goin', get a couple items done,
Instead of just enjoyin life
Beneath this autumn sun.

Now I sit here just staring at this pretty countryside,
The river runnin' past me,
That eagle in the sky.

I think I'll sit and ponder and not really give a damn.
If you think that you may need me,
I'll be here just ponderin'.

The Gathering

Photo by Paul Buol

Photo by Michael Whitaker

Weitis

W ell, it all started out on Weitis Creek
    a couple years ago.
The country a little steeper
    than the maps ever dared to show.

And, boy, in the spring time,
    when the winter snows would run.
The rocks would roll down Weitis Creek,
    tumblin' one by one.

The outfitter down on Weitis Creek
    had picked him up a pup.
The dog didn't even have a name.
    Seems a name just didn't come up.

He had his share of dogs and mules
    and the horses that he owned.
He knew that he would have to find
    this young pup a brand new home.

One day he swung by Jay's Ranch,
    the ol' Lazy Rockin' "J".
The pup jumped out of the truck
    and rubbed against Jay's leg.

The outfitter knew the deal was sealed,
    it was a blessing in disguise.
He knew he had found this pup a home,
    you could see it in Jay's eyes.

The pup and Jay just hit it off
    like a couple of long-lost friends.
Folks, this is quite a story,
    and this is where it all begins.

The pup, he grew a foot or two,
    and would run around the clock.
But ya should have seen ol' Jay's face
    when the pup started rollin' rocks.

Clear up on the hillside
    the rocks came tumblin' down.
They echoed down the canyon,
    and could be heard for miles around.

Ol' Jay he called his buddy,
    and inquired about his skills,
As he stared out at that young dog,
    that was rollin' rocks from off the hill.

The outfitter asked if he was good,
    and if he was acting tame.
Ol' Jay said that he was doing fine,
    but does the dog even have a name?

He replied "I'd call him Weitis,
    Ya know, the creek I outfit on.
Weitis Creek runs straight down hill,
    and the rocks roll all day long."

Jay just hung the phone up,
    and leaned against the window sill,
Just staring out at Weitis
    That was rollin' rocks from off the hill.

When I tell folks of ol' Weitis
    they just don't know what to say.
It's a story that I'll pack with me,
    until my dying days.

So if you're ever around Kamiah,
    and have some time you'd like to kill,
Just come and watch ol' Weitis,
    roll those rocks from off the hill.

To Jay and Weitis

White Creek

Buried back in the hills on the middle fork of the Salmon
   are places that very few see.
There are hidden treasures scattered all across this land,
   scattered with old memories.

Photo by Michael Whitaker

Don't know the stories, best that I don't.
   Just leave them there on their own.
Reminisce of time, an unforgivin' life,
   a simple way that was known.

About five or six mile up White Creek
   sits a cabin from long ago.
The windows are gone, the roof has collapsed,
   No doors, no sign of a stove.

The logs that are stacked to make her walls
    are old and weathered white.
But I bet back then she was a sight to see
    on a cold Idaho night.

White Creek runs next to her.
    It runs the year around.
The ridge that runs right above her
    has golden grass 'cross the ground.

She's just nestled in the pine trees,
    a perfect spot to be.
Now nature has won this on-goin' battle,
    she's just a faded memory.

Well, I paused for a bit, took an hour or two,
    just sat and leaned against her walls.
I watched the deer up on that golden ridge,
    enjoyed the timber tall.

The mice and squirrels now make her home;
    the old girl is quite a sight.
But ya can't help but think of the fire that burned
    in that stove on a cold snowy night.

An old cabin sittin' on White Creek
    underneath a ridge of gold.
Memories hangin' in the timber,
    many stories left untold.

Winter Moon

There are many signs of winter;
   like the turning of the leaves,
The hair so thick on a horses hide,
   the chill in the autumn breeze.

But tonight he knows by morning
   the ice will cover that ol' ground.
He can tell by that White Moon
   that's so bright and oh, so round.

When the moon is crystal white,
   he knows that she'll be getting cold.
So cold it will freeze your hide
   right down to your very soul.

He'll build a fire right next to him,
   and stack the wood so high.
Why he lives here in this country,
   I simply don't know the reason why.

How the elk survive here
   is a mystery to us all.
The air so cold you can cut it.
   The wolves they cry their call.

The ice builds upon the streams;
   the trees turn icy white.
The ground reflects like diamonds,
   on this cold winter's night.

That ol' bag keeps him pretty warm
    even though she's been around.
Under him horse blankets scattered
    to protect him from the frozen ground.

The night, she lasts forever.
    He wakes with a face so cold,
He pulls his head on under
    this old and wore out roll.

The night turns into morning;
    the ground, she starts to steam.
His eyes open one by one.
    His head is full of dreams.

The sun, she breaks the hilltops.
    He makes himself a pot.
The morning fire feels good to him.
    The fire is burning hot.

The sun now shines across his face.
    Boy, does it feels good.
Man is not made for winter.
    It is somethin' that's understood.

He packs up the mules and his ol' horse,
    he heads on down the trail.
Just an average night on Big Creek,
    just a simple Cowboy's tale.

Fire Storm

Sitting next to Big Creek are cabins and some sheds.
The fellow that takes care of her is a man they call Big Red.
He lives with his wife there; they moved there long ago.
The only time I met him was up on Cliff Creek in the snow.

Taylor Ranch is simple, with a bridge that spans Big Creek.
Not a bunch to do there but they make the best of it.
One day surely changed their lives; it was hot and dry that year.
The brush was fuel for makin' and fire they did fear.

Then the storms came their way; lightning struck the ground.
Fires broke out everywhere, they could hear that deadly sound.
Days passed one by one, they watched with every breath.
Kept an eye on every hillside; they seldom got to rest.

One day the wind did change; the fire came rushing down.
It raced down the hillsides and for them it was surely bound.
They gathered up just what they could and loaded up the mules.
Left in a full out hurry before they were known as fools.

Headin' straight down Big Creek with the fire right behind.
They wondered when they returned just what they would find.
The cabins and the buildings were now left on their own.
Stayin' alive one more day; hoping that they would make it home.

But just when the smoke cleared and the pressure slowly seized.
They ran into a big maw bear; she had her young cubs up a tree.
Wondered what else could go wrong, they talked to this old gal.
They tried and tried to tell her that everything was well.

That old maw bear understood listened to her friends.
Grabbed her cubs and headed up the hill, never to be seen again.

Up the Middle Fork this couple slowly made their way.
They headed for the Flying "B". It is there they now would stay.
They told them of the fires and the direction of the wind.
They knew that fire was on its way that they would meet again.

The hands and this couple cleaned the brush around the place.
Tired and surely worn out, from such a heavy pace.
Then a rumble from up the canyons, echoed through the air.
They all ran for the river. You could smell the fear.

The fire raced down the canyons at speeds too fast for them.
They cut the fences, chased the mules; thought it was the end.
They ducked beneath the water; the fire flew over head.
One by one they surfaced, to see if they were dead.

But all was fine that day of days. The cowboys looked around.
The timber burnt and shattered; now everyone was found.
The couple returned to Taylor Ranch, wondered what was there.
A bunk house or two was missin', but the rest was standin' fair.

Now the fire that went down Big Creek left nothin' much behind.
Red is still livin' there and Taylor Ranch is lookin' fine.
Within eight miles of Taylor, I couldn't bear to go that way.
I knew if I saw him eye to eye, I wouldn't know just what to say.

If you're ever around the Flying "B" or near Old Taylor Ranch.
It will explain the ways of nature and the simple game of chance.

The Perfect Hunt

Twenty years we've been together, trying to hunt the beast,
Traveling state by state, half the world at least.

We've hunted across high deserts up the mountainsides,
Just me and my oid buddy always hunting side by side.

But the biggest thrill we're looking for never turns out right.
We try and try everyday but are failures every night.

For twenty years our hunts have been somewhat of a success.
But way down low we both do know it's really not the best.

We prepare like no others, we plan and plan again.
But as we almost get our prey, we lose and never win.

A few years back we had it and it somehow slipped away.
Knew we'd have another shot, there would be another day.

Some men would have given up but we knew we had to try
Why we do just what we do, I'll never know the reason why.

Our attempts have taken us high and low and everywhere in-between.
But for now, we must accept that it will only be a dream.

As the situation rises we hold our breath and pray
But when we think we have it our dream just fades away.

The Gathering

It must be the temperature, too hot our just too cold.
Our strategies have failed us, sometimes I just don't know.

We've tried to be real quiet, we've tried to yell and scream.
We've tried a hundred different ways but they never do succeed.

But this year our hopes of winning were at the very top.
The climate was just perfect, not too cold or too hot.

We both took our positions, we crouched and sat so still.
Anticipation overwhelmed us, we simply love the thrill.

The tension grew like a big balloon and the moment grew so near.
We could hear it making noises—a sound that's, oh, so dear.

We sat, watched and waited. My nerves they grew so thin.
My heart pounded rapidly, my face displayed a grin.

After years it finally happened. There it lays in front of me.
Our Jiffy-Pop™ popped all the way. Our lives are now complete.

Photo by Buzz Bickler

Chapter 3
Montana

Photo by Buzz Bickler

Montana

Montana is a land of raw beauty, kind people and foreverness. In some areas it is just remote enough that ya best know where you are going and someone best know where ya went.

The history of this land runs deep with cowboys who took a chance, a real chance, basically on life itself. Too far to ship cattle, too cold to raise them in the winter, but the summers make up for it all, if it rains enough in the spring.

When ya take the time to go to small towns like Stanford, Grass Range, Moore, Utica and all the rest. Take time to sit and talk with the ranchers and farmers; it is then you will know Montana. When a Cowboy walks through the door wearin' a bandanna it's not because it looks good but rather because it keeps the cold winter wind off his neck when he's herdin' up cattle. Oh yes, they still use horses.

You know a Montana cowboy when ya see them; hat, bandanna, tight coat, long thin build, high boots to the knees (the kind that ya can wash the gumbo off), and a flatbed truck with a trailer behind it, horses already saddled standin' in the back. Don't say a lot, but polite and respectable. Think maybe the quietness comes from the cold winter wind or livin' a little too far from town for too many years.

There's a family I know from an area called Danvers. Danvers is a little town with two grain elevators, a school, church and a train track running through it. The town is mostly gone now, but there still are a few farmhouses scattered about where wheat is still growing tall. The one thing that got the best of me the last time I visited Danvers was what I found in the cemetery. It was the generations of folks buried there, folks from Danvers. If you know someone buried there you know they came from a place of remoteness, cold winter days, gumbo, and hailstorms that can ruin a years work in the matter of hours. The Tucek family came from Danvers. Why they lived here I just don't know. I guess that can be asked of many people and I guess the answer is that it is just who they are and where they came from.

Where they came from is Montana.

North Plains

The winter sun sits on the edge.
   The clouds are rolling in.
The evening was sitting quietly;
   you could feel the winter wind.

Stretched across the horizon,
   the cloud an inch from the cold ground.

The outline of the Buttes
   could be seen from miles around.
There's a ranch out in the distance;
   the lights are dim and few.

The ol' ranch shows history,
   a time I wish I knew.
The north plains of Montana,
   a land I've come to love.

The winter's moon ashining
   with the lanterns up above.
I looked in all directions,
   there was not a soul in sight.

I stood there in the nothingness,
   on that cold November night.
It's a land where prickly pear fight for sun,
   a land where the cold wind blows.

Saw an ol' steer's skull just lying there
   in a grassy patch of snow.
A strange and desperate land I see,
   a story that takes time.

The Gathering

The north plains of Montana,
   a rare and honest find.
The miles go on forever,
   a land where few belong.

The north plains of Montana
   singing a cold and timeless song.

Photo by Michael Whitaker

There's Somethin'

There's somethin' that I left behind;
　　what it is I just don't know.
Maybe the Judith Mountains
　　trimmed with a foot or two of snow.

Could be the Lower Moccasins,
　　the Crazy's or the Belts.
There's somethin' that I left behind.
　　It's a strange feelin' I can't help.

It may be that big bull elk
　　I spotted off the breaks.
Could be that big ol' settin' sun,
　　the one shinin' off the lake.

Maybe that age ol' cowboy;
　　that night we talked for hours.
Can't put my finger on it
　　even though I've scoured and scoured.

I feel as though I've left behind,
　　somethin' that's worth a lot.
I wish I knew just what it is
　　or just what I forgot.

But for now I'll have to ponder,
　　think back a day or two.
Back to those times I enjoyed myself
　　underneath a sky of blue.

The Gathering

It somehow has got the best of me,
    not knowin' what it is.
I somehow can't remember.
    In my mind I can't relive.

Could be the friendly folks I met.
    Could be the rancher's wave.
Could be the never-ending roads.
    Could be the rocks and sage.

But when I think back to what it is
    all I see are pretty hills.
Only thought that comes across my mind
    is the beauty this land fills.

The wind that waves through fields of grain,
    the mountains just above.
The antelope that pepper the landscape;
    this land I truly love.

The rolling fields of winter wheat
    as far as you can see.
The colors of this rugged mass
    takes my breath away from me.

So it will have to stay a mystery,
    these unsolved thoughts I find.
Until I'm back in ol' Montana,
    maybe then it will come to mind.

Danvers Montana

In the desolate land of wheat fields and farms
 where the land is flat and bare.
The men and women have a way about them
 in their eyes, their smiles that care.

They can say so much without speaking a word.
 You can write a book on a glance.
This way they have comes from the wind and the snow
 and livin' nowhere on a ranch.

It's a place where winters never forgive,
 and the sun burns the mud into dust.
The wheat grows high, the grain flows gold,
 the clay is filled with rust.

These gifts that they have come from sage brush, snakes,
 that butte that sits all alone,
A run down farm house, a weathered barn roof,
 the place they know as home.

Just because they're quiet
 doesn't mean they have no minds.
They know what they're doin', what they're pursuin';
 they just do it in their own time.

If you just don't see or quite understand
 what these folks are trying to say,
Just move to a town called Danvers, Montana,
 and soon you'll be talkin' this way.

A Town Beneath The Mountains

Oh, this town here lies abandoned
The rest was hauled away

The stories that this town once told
Just drift across the plains

The school house still is standin',
Not used for many years

The church that sits across the road,
Her bell you seldom hear

I heard back then she was quite a town
When harvest was complete.

The elevators filled to the top,
Trains loadin' golden wheat

A harvest dance or two were held,
They'd come from miles around

But the folks don't dance anymore
In this forgotten old wheat town

The farms they still sit about.
The wheat still grows so high.

This little town sits quietly.
Don't know the reason why.

The cemetery is kept up well
In honor of the few.

The people that started this treasure,
The town that we once knew

The mountains in the distance
Keep watch on her they say.

Keep watch on the folks that live here,
Folks tendin' wheat and fightin' clay.

A way of life that few can bear,
A life of golden charm.

A town beneath the mountains,
Its people and their farms.

I stood there on that November day
I could not bear to go.

A small town they call Danvers.
A small church kneeling in the snow.

Photo by Michael Whitaker

Danvers, Montana

Painted Snow

Like artwork on a gallery wall
   the snow covers him with paint.
His head is tucked upon his chin;
   his image cold and faint.

He hears a cow a bawlin'
   from the far side of the ridge.
He rides a beeline for her
   to see what help that he may give.

The late snow shouldn't be here;
   too far within the year.
The wind is howlin' across the snow.
   it's cold and so sincere.

He looks ahead to see them,
   the snow creates a blur.
He taps his horse with his two heels
   then gently speaks a word.

He rides upon that cry for help
   and there lies a withered calf.
He gently eyes the cow he sees
   and begins a daunting task.

He strokes the shivered calf a bit.
   He'll save it if he can.
There becomes an understandin'
   between that old cow and the man.

The Gathering

He grabs a coat from his saddle,
    wraps it nice and neat.
Across his lap this calf does ride,
    a shiverin' hide and hangin' feet.

The cow somehow understands,
    just walks along behind.
The snow comes down upon them.
    It's a spring with winter skies.

Some may think he is a hero,
    the manners of a saint,
Just ridin' down a cattle trail
    covered with white paint.

A painting of a way of life,
    a verse of a ranchers song,
A cowboy with a freezing calf,
    a cow following along.

He shelters both the calf and cow,
    he puts his horse away.
Just another day of ranchin'
    on a cold and snowy day.

Like art work on a gallery wall,
    the snow covers him with paint.
He walks on towards an ol' ranch house,
    his image cold and faint.

Eddies's Corner

It was years ago when I first stopped in
   for a beer and a bite to eat.

An old classic bar, in the middle of nowhere
   with a pot bellied stove for heat.

Beer was a buck, whiskey was a quarter more.
   The music was a roll of the dice.

It was a haven, a home, a place to stop by
   out of the cold wind and the ice.

The family that owned it was friendly as hell.
   The meals they served were great.

Not a four star restaurant by any means,
   but their steaks hung over the plate.

If the first plate didn't fill you up,
   they'd grab and do it again.

Through the years of stoppin' and sayin' "Hi,"
   I knew I was known as a friend.

But the biggest impression the bar made on me
   was a sign that I failed to mention.

Hangin' over the bar, it simply read,
   "Booze is the answer, what was the question?"

To the Bauman Family

Eddie's Corner is located in the small town of Moore, Montana. It sits exactly halfway between where you're goin' or where you're comin' from. If ya need somethin' to eat, they've got it; a shower, they've got it; a beer, they've got that, too. If ya need directions, just pull out a map of Montana and look for the dead center of the state, it will read Moore. If your wonderin' what hours they keep, come anytime. They've never closed in fifty years.

Eddie's Corner, 1954

Carryin' On

The boots are scattered inside the door,
   the coats hang on the rack.
The cobwebs line the porch walls,
   there sits a bob tailed cat.

The fly strip hangs from the light above.
   It's as cold as you can find.
It's an old ranch out on the open plains
   just lettin' time slip by.

The kitchen smells like fresh baked bread.
   The supper's waitin' on the stove.
There's a table that's sittin' eight cowboys.
   They serve it up before its cold.

But before they take a single bite
   they bow their heads and close their eyes.
It's an old ranch out on the open plains
   just lettin' time slip by.

They head to bed real early.
   The morning comes too soon.
They'll have a day's work put away
   before the clock strikes noon.

The old boys know no better.
   It's the way they live their lives.
It's an old ranch out on the plains
   just lettin' time slip by.

The Gathering

Time, it surely changes things.
    The youngest boys move to town.
But the eldest boy he stays behind;
    it's the only life he's found.

Pa, he just can't get around.
    Ma, she sits inside.
But ranchin' it still carries on.
    It becomes a thing of pride.

Workin' hands are hard to find.
    There ain't good ones anymore.
The few that he keeps on
    are reminded of their chores.

But ranchin's in this young man's blood,
    a tradition he keeps alive.
It's an old ranch out on the open plains
    just lettin' time slip by.

If it ain't the cold harsh winters,
    it is the beatin' sun.
The money from the banker,
    the loans that carry on.

The drought that seems to never end,
    the cost the ranch now takes.
Sometime it gets right to him—
    a bit more then he can make.

So he saddles up his pony
    He takes himself a ride.
He heads up to the high ground
    to see the spaces wide.

The colors of the waving land,
    the coulees just below.
The deer across the canyon,
    a life he's come to know.

The setting sun before him,
    the silhouetted hills.
This land has a certain beauty.
    His heart now overfills.

It reminds him why he lives here,
    the hard and endless fight.
He would never trade a single day.
    He now understands his father's life.

He knows there is no better.
    He knows the reasons and the whys.
Just a rancher out on the open plains
    just lettin' time slip by.

Photo by Michael Whitaker

Farmhouse on Montana Plains

Square Butte

I have always liked the flatlands,
   the sun just burning down.
The big old sky looking down on me.
   You can see for miles around.

But all the things I've seen in my life,
   there is one I hold so dear—
A Butte that watches over me
   as I live my life each year.

Square Butte just a standin'
   as proud as she can be.
Never been to the top of her;
   it has always been a dream.

I wonder what it's like up there,
   I bet you could see forever.
She is pretty in the summer sun,
   in the spring and snowy weather.

Every time I go her way,
   I can not help but gaze.
She just looks down upon me,
   as I slowly live my days.

I have seen her in the paintings,
   I have seen her in real life.
I have seen her in the light of day,
   silhouetted by moonlight.

Photo by Michael Whitaker

Square Butte, Montana

Every time I look at her
   she is staring back at me.
A weathered face with rugged rocks,
   cliffs so tall and steep.

I wonder what the settlers thought
   when she first came in sight—
Standing in her glory,
   strong and full of might.

The Indians must worship her.
   She must be sacred ground.
At night if you listen close
   you can hear those haunting sounds.

To think that ice had carved her
   from the molten rock,
Left the world laying at her feet,
   a place that time's forgot.

I wonder who it was that named her.
   I would have like to met that man.
To ask him what he thought—
   a Butte that is so grand.

Some forget she is even there
   as they live beneath her cliffs.
It is sad that they do not take the time.
   Her grandeur is surely missed.

When I die just lay me down
   where the heavens come in view.
A place that I have been dreaming of—
   the top of "Old Square Butte."

Flatwillow

In the middle of Montana there is a land I've come to know.
Half way down a valley where the pace is nice and slow.

Just one town to mark her, one church, an abandoned school.
The folks that came to call 'er home are but very few.

This land is like a storybook, the houses lean, so old.
The air is filled with history and stories left untold.

But it has a certain beauty, a beauty of its own.
In the middle of Montana there is a land I've come to know.

If your headin' out of Grass Range take a right on Three Mile Hill.
Head down towards the valley, the one the willows fill.

You will be in the Flatwillow with a creek that runs her length.
It meanders slow and steady. She seldom leaves her banks.

Up at the headwaters there is a corral from long ago.
I stood there one winter's day in a foot or two of snow.

The snow stacked on the rails of this corral of many years.
I could her the cattle bawlin', the crying of the steers.

It was a thought in winter silence; it was a thought from long ago.
Just me and the Flatwillow with a heavy coat of snow.

I wonder just how life was in the cattle herdin' days
When the days were filled with sunshine, the chasin' of the strays.

When the tumblin' of the water overflows into your soul.
Your eyes soon close so heavy, with the summer moon aglow.

To most this is just a valley and a creek that runs its course.
A place to summer range the cattle and a place to ride their horse.

But I can see the weathered barns and corrals of long ago.
A place called the Flatwillow with a creek that runs so slow.

A sky that runs forever, with grass so tall and green,
Where meadows meet the mountains, the air is crisp and clean.

So if you're lookin' for me and a creek that runs so slow,
I'll be in the middle of Montana, a land I've come to know.

Photo by Michael Whitaker

Flatwillow, Montana

Just A Feeling

This country changes most folks.
　　Life slows down to a crawl.
Fields run on forever.
　　Really not much here at all.

The sun bakes down upon the fields.
　　At night the moon does shine.
Someday I think I'll make a move,
　　slow down the hands of time.

Ya know, it's just a feeling.
　　It sneaks upon me when I come this way.
When I'm headed back for home
　　I think I'd rather stay.

Ya know it's just a feeling.
　　It gets stronger every year.
Think a change is now in order.
　　Pack up and move back here.

Convenience is real hard to find.
　　Need does take its place.
Kind heartiness is a way of life.
　　These folks invented grace.

The Cowboy way is here to stay.
　　It's not something that they planned.
It was passed on down from their great grandpas,
　　the homesteaders of this land.

The Gathering

Ya know it's just a feeling
    when the red sun starts to set.
When the day is through and the sky is blue,
    life has not one regret.

Ya know it's just a feeling,
    the changing of ones' mind—
A land so bold it will move your soul,
    a peace that's hard to find.

The history of this sun-burnt land
    is recorded in the hills.
The shear rock cliffs just lookin' down
    across the old wheat fields.

The simple wave that comes your way
    from a rancher in his truck.
A sweaty brow and callused hands—
    Success didn't come from luck.

Ya know it's just a feeling
    I simply can't ignore.
I have to trust this heart of mine.
    I'm not waitin' anymore.

So my friend, I must move on.
    I owe it to myself.
I'm headed for a new way of life,
    a new book upon life's shelf.

Leanin' Fences

The Montana sky never lies
    when the north wind comes around.
The blues turn white, there's geese in flight,
    It's time shelter should be found.
But a couple strays had made their way
    in a coulee just below.
They don't get around real well
    when their bellies drag the snow.

A quarter horse now takes a course
    down a long and slippery bank.
They creep on down, some footings found,
    the deep snow they both can thank.
The skies they are a changin'.
    The north wind starts to blow.
The wind cuts through his memories.
    Best move 'em on towards home.

Across the flats, he snugs his hat.
    the wind and snow prevail.
Not a thing in sight, the air is white,
    they no longer see a trail.
Direction is real hard to find.
    He relies upon his wits.
They ride for hours in the snowy air
    tryin' to make some sense of it.

His head he lifts as the snow does drift
    a leanin' fence is found.
He's feelin' right. It's a welcome site
    for this is familiar ground.

He rides that leanin' fence line.
    They make their way back home.
There, out in the distance
    sits a ranch house all alone.
Faith is a friend in the northern winds
    when you're relyin' on a prayer.
When strays are found on the lower ground,
    the snow does fill the air.

Flat lands and the blowin' snow
    don't mix by any means.
Life was hangin' pretty hard
    on a rusty fence that leans.
He had some thoughts of the snow he fought,
    and some jobs he didn't do
When the grass was green and his time was lean,
    the things he never did pursue.

A job he had no time for,
    the one that never did commence.
The tearin' down of that ol' eye sore,
    that rusty leanin' fence.

Photo by Michael Whitaker

Chapter 4
Home Fire

My mother Frances Whitaker in her younger days

Friends and Family

I've had some remarkable things go in my favor the last few years. Some may say it's luck, but I know it's the people around me. When I think of the important things in life all I see are kind and loving faces. In the fast pace ways of the world we now live in, I know if it weren't for family and friends it would all come undone.

History is important to me and, at times, maybe most of the time, I live in the past. I have included a poem of my dad's family migration. It was a bit of a challenge finding the history and events. With my dad and grandparents now passed all I had were bits and pieces Then. about six months ago I stumbled across an ol' wooden box of my grandmother's and found photos of my dad when he was young. Included was my grandmother's family journal, which filled in all of the blanks. Needless to say, it was quite a find.

My mother and I spent a Saturday together and reminisced the day away. When I'm eighty-three, I hope I can recall as well as she. Mom took me back to her childhood, the hard times and good times. The long trip to Washington and the year she met my dad. This has been one of the biggest enjoyments while putting this book together.

I have had a lot of fun writing about friends and some of the situations I have shared with them. With friends like mine, I usually have a lot of things to write about. They seem to be gettin' a little gun shy though. Whenever someone screws up I normally hear, "You're not goin' to write about this are you?" Bein' the good friend that I am, I lie and just tell them, "No."

This chapter of the book is almost all true. Well, let's call it "semi-nonfiction."

Photo by unknown family member

My dad at 12 years old.

Sand Creek

Our blood is splattered across this land
   they traveled in those days;
From the flat plains of Nebraska,
   to a town known as St. James.

In Missouri my grandpa was an ol' auctioneer.
   Hear those auction sounds?
I can still see and hear him.
   A new life they now had found.

Then they moved west to Wyoming,
   land of golden wheat.
It was a cattle ranch where they found their home,
   a place known as Sand Creek.

Sand Creek lies south of Laramie,
   just north of the Colorado line.
My dad was just a young man then,
   a place way back in time.

Mitch Bert Vetter was the ranch boss.
   head honcho of "Cook Ranch."
He'd let my dad ride with 'em;
   my dad was glad he got the chance.

It was there my granddad got hurt.
   He would never walk again.
It happened while bustin' a young horse.
   They thought it was the end.

He landed on a cactus.
    It stuck him in the spine.
He sat there in his wheel chair
    until the end of time.

Why they then moved out to Oregon,
    I guess I'll never know.
A long ways from Wyoming
    where ol' Sand Creek slowly flows.

My dad did work the lumber mills.
    My grandpa worked his wood.
He'd carve and lathe bowls and such,
    made a livin' as he could.

My dad headed up to Washington.
    That's where he met my mom.
Bought a home to raise a family,
    a nice place to carry on.

Now Buckley is a small town.
    That is where I now reside.
A small town up in Washington—
    in the foothills it does hide.

My folks moved here quite long ago,
    when logging was in steam.
They lived here 'til his dyin' day.
    It was here they filled their dreams.

But he'd talk about Wyomin',
    the cattle herdin' days.
By a mountain fire, he'd sit and stare,
    talk of the wranglin' ways.

He was fond of the Cowboy life,
    a life that he once had.
Lives that were so simple,
    the lives of my grandfather and my dad.

Oscar Whitaker

Reliable and Practical

AUCTIONEER

GUARANTEED SATISFACTION

St. James, Mo.

*Make Dates at Powell Lumber Company
or the Journal Office.*

Photo by unknown family member

My dad at eight-years-old

An Ol' Six-String

Too young to really understand
　what he held within his hands.
An old six-string that was handed down,
　out of tune and soundin' bland.

But he sat there upon that wooden box,
　would play for hours and hours.
Tryin' to reach his fingerings,
　his memory he would scour.

He grew up playing music.
　His audience was small at best.
He sang those old time cowboy songs,
　the ones of the rugged west.

When I had come to know him
　he hardly played at all.
But I liked to hear his singin',
　"Ridin' down the Canyon" most of all.

Sometimes I'd hear him playing,
　by himself there all alone.
I'd listen to those ol' time songs,
　how he'd yodel, how he'd moan.

It started from a wooden box,
　a young boy and his guitar,
An old time faded photograph
　and memories from afar.

I have his guitar hid away.
    I'll grab it now and then.
It gives me a real good feelin',
    like I'm holdin' a dear old friend.

Then I see a young boy clear as day
    on an ol' Nebraska Ranch.
No shoes upon his filthy feet,
    no sign of hope or chance.

His dreams just laid upon his lap,
    it's all this young boy had.
My life has been much easier
    than the life of dear ol' dad.

My mom wishes I could play like him,
    make that six-string ring.
But I know it's just her missin' him,
    and the ol' songs that he would sing.

It started from a wooden box,
    a young boy with feet so bare;
An old time faded photograph,
    a few memories we now share.

I stumbled across an old wood box that was filled with old photos and such that belonged to my grandmother. In the box I found some old photos of my dad and my grandfather. Each photo had how old my dad was. With a journal that my grandmother kept I could match up just where they were taken. Some of these photos are priceless. Thought I'd share a couple.

Our youngest son has always been full of surprises. The first surprise was to come into this world sixteen weeks too early. At one pound, six ounces he was not much bigger than a minute. He had quite a struggle but had all of the will in the world. His name fits him to a tee and "Will" hasn't changed a bit. At a time like this you realize how important mothers are. Will picked the best mom in the world—my dear wife Judy. You know that you have a good mom when she dedicates her whole life to you. Judy certainly does that with each and every one of our children.

My mom is exactly the same way. All that she has done for all of her kids could never be paid back. When I think of my mom, I have thoughts of her canning beans, making butter, open toed white sandals, but most of all, her rocking babies and singing that familiar song that she always sings. This next poem is about my mom's life and was written just for her.

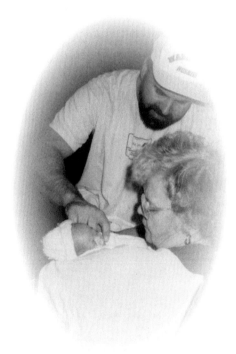

Photo by Judy Whitaker

Mom, Will and myself.

201

Songs of the Past

North of Crandon a couple miles
   is where my mom came from.
On a road that they call Range Line,
   in the hot Wisconsin sun.

My mom, she went to school there.
   It was the place where she was raised.
Her brothers and her sisters
   learnt how to work and how to play.

She tells of the winter nights
   by the stove they'd mend and darn.
Her mother rocked sweet Donna,
   sang to her in her arms.

She'd sing "Little Orphan Annie."
   The kids would listen in.
They didn't have a lot then—
   the only life they had to live.

It would snow and drift all winter,
   stack upon the trees.
Each and every Christmas
   her father made them skis.

In the long and sultry summers,
   at the creek they all would swim.
They didn't have a lot then—
   the only life they had to live.

The Gathering

When my mom was nearing twenty
   her family pulled up stakes.
They headed out to Washington
   where money could be made.

Two ol' covered flatbeds,
   their belongings, clothes and kids,
Leaving dear ol' Range Line,
   the place that they once lived.

The trip was long and taxing,
   got separated on the way.
In Deer Lodge they were stranded.
   Somehow they went astray.

Left with little money,
   Uncle Louie hawked his gun.
They headed out all on their own
   for that final run.

Carbonado would be their new home.
   The men worked in the woods.
My mom, she worked many jobs,
   made a living as she could.

She started working in the shipyards;
   first woman ship-fitter in this land.
The shipyards would change her life.
   It was there she met my dad.

They settled up above South Prairie.
   Then a home was bought in small Burnett.
It was there my two sisters and I
   were raised with no regrets.

We lived there through my high school days
    until we lost our dad.
A time I won't soon forget,
    a time I'm glad I had.

But I remember when I was little,
    and in that rocking chair.
My mom would hold and rock me,
    chase away my fears.

Little things stay with you.
    I don't know the reason why.
But I can still hear her singing,
    "By Oh Baby By."

To My Dear Mother

Photo by Mike Twardoski

My Mom Frances Whitaker and great granddaughter Caitlyn.

Painted Horse

A Blaze Face and a new Paint Horse
    traveling down a familiar course,
Pine trees and a meadow filled with snow,
    the sunshine across the cold.

Things are new to our Painted friend.
    Ears perk up, it's just a winter wind.
Mister's been down this trail many times before.
    A shadow's thrown as a hawk soars.

The boys ride side by side,
    many memories they can not hide.
Remember what they were way back when;
    Now is now and that was then.

The mountain lends us a few good days.
    A storm comes and takes it all away.
Give us sun and fresh fallen snow.
    Saddle up for a winter stroll.

Amigo starts to settle down,
    A new life has been found.
Mister leads as they head for a ride.
    Amigo knows that this is fine.

A Blaze Face and a Painted Horse,
    both know this familiar course.
Life is good as the sun shines across the snow.
    Saddle up for a winter stroll.

The history of the Paints is long
   like the sounds of the winter song.
A Brave rides the Paint in the Aspen trees.
   You can look but you'll never see.

Photo by Mike Twardoski

The blood runs thick and is true as time.
   The Paint's proud and a rare find.
As thick as blood has ever ran,
   is true for the horse and is true for man.

Uncle Mike

Once Again

I'm not sure of the reason it came across my mind,
   I was mindin' to myself.
It was just like stumblin' across a good ol' book
   just sittin' upon the shelf.

The memories came a flowin'.
   They kept comin' all day long.
Just like a visit from a long lost friend
   or a good ol' country song.

I haven't had these thoughts for years.
   In a way I felt ashamed.
The times we had way back when
   will never be the same.

But times we had, none the less,
   now they're just old memories.
Back in the good ol' days,
   how life's supposed to be.

My ol' man and I would go riding,
   way back in the hills.
We'd fish 'til the sun went down,
   then eat 'til we had our fill.

He would cuss, laugh and would tell his lies,
   but ya know, I didn't mind.
In the world we now are livin',
   men like him are hard to find.

He always was teachin' me,
    and at times he drove me crazy.
If you planned on being 'round him much
    ya better not be lazy.

When it came to doin' most anything,
    there was a one and only way.
I think this teachin' somehow's been lost.
    We need it back, I'd have to say.

Now I don't mean to say he was ornery.
    He had a heart of gold.
He took time for me and most everyone
    that stumbled down his road.

He's been gone most of my life,
    I still have a few things of his.
I shoulda had kept just one more.
    At my age it's surely missed.

I can see it plain as day, although
    it was old and half wore out.
Just to sit upon her once again
    is what I dream about.

He died when I was way too young.
    I just didn't understand.
Now I wish I had that saddle,
    the one that belonged to my ol' man.

To My Ol' Man

Photo by Nick Whitaker

There's a happy ending to this poem. I wrote this poem several years back and sent a copy to my Uncle Bill. He gave me a call and let me know that he had my dad's saddle all along. The saddle now sits in my barn and on occasion it has my Ol' Man's kid sittin' right in the middle of 'er. Thanks for everything, Bill.

The Way It Is

You can tell just by the way they talk
    that these cowboys are more than friends.
You know that when it came right down to it
    they'd be there 'til the bitter end.

They know when to help, know when to step back;
    it's somethin' that's done without words.
It's a thing ya can't teach or even preach.
    It's a way that's seen, but never heard.

We found my Uncle's horse bedded down,
    his front leg was in real bad shape.
His leg drug on the ground. He hobbled on down.
    It was a bit more than most men can take.

We fed him some hay and watered him up,
    called the Vet for a better way.
The Vet shook his head said somethin' he dreads.
    Wasn't much more the man could say.

The Cowboys did stand to gave my uncle a hand
    with a job they knew they were bound.
See, there was no savin' this young Quarter Horse.
    The only way was to put him down.

One by one they stepped in to help,
    with a chore they would rather not do.
It's a thing ya can't teach or even preach.
    It's a way that is honest and true.

They laugh and they cuss, they drink a bit much,
    but ya know when a man's a true friend.
When it come to strife, the tough side of life,
    there will be standin' these few honest men.

Photo by Mike Twardoski

My youngest boy, Will, was with us when we found the horse. Seems the horse had taken a bad fall and broken his shoulder. Will was pretty young when he found out about the tough side of being a Cowboy.

To Uncle Bill, Jay, Ron & Russ

Old Walls

It's been quite a spell, I'm here to tell,
    the last time I've stepped through these doors.
The place is old and it's down right cold.
    The hand-made rug still lies on the floor.

You could spend most of the day just gazin' away
    at the old pictures that hang from the walls.
It's nice in the winter when you shiver and shimmer,
    but I like it most here in the fall.

The big potbelly stove just standin' so bold,
    warms the chill from the air in this room.
I'll dust off the chairs, sweep down the stairs
    with this old worn-out wicker broom.

Then I'll get to doing and start pursuing
    something that's most dear to me.
Pull out my pen, a fine old friend,
    and start writin' my poetry.

The sun slips behind; the day comes to a grind,
    and the room turns into a dream.
The words start to rhyme from this crippled old mind,
    formin' words of an ol' western scene.

A glass of Merlot, warms this body and soul,
    and it helps me put life into words.
A cabin of old is where I bare my soul
    just puttin' words into verse.

It's a thing I must tell of this world where I dwell.
Words come easy when the leaves start to fall.
A small cabin in the woods, where life's understood,
and old memories just hang from the walls.

Photo by Michael Whitaker

Backside

It's funny how things change
   as the years do pass on by.
Things as you get older—
   can't explain the reasons why.

I remember as a kid
   I thought that things were bigger than they are.
Thought that most places were a million miles away,
   but they really weren't that far.

At the age of ten most folks thought
   I was shy and liked to hide.
'Cause most of the time you would find me,
   right at my ol' man's backside.

Wherever he would wander,
   at his backside I would be.
Usually by a campfire
   next to a mountain steam.

If it weren't for his ol' backside
   I wouldn't have got too far.
Wouldn't have got to know him'
   or ever seen the mountain stars .

They often called me "Shadow".
   See, I didn't understand.
I was usually just a standin' there
   at the backside of my ol' man.

When we would go aridin'
    you'd find me trailing right behind
Just a staring at hillsides.
    A better life would be hard to find.

You can learn a lot from your ol' man
    if you take the time to watch.
The places that he takes you,
    the way he walks and talks.

So if life gets a bit confusin',
    and ya just don't understand.
Just remember the ways of the good ol' days,
    at the backside of your ol' man.

A Long Gravel Road

I remember the picnics our families had,
    my aunts, uncles, my mom and dad.
You know life really wasn't all that bad,
    down our long gravel road.

When the summer sun burnt down on us,
    out by the barn we would play and cuss.
We would drive an old tractor that was all covered with rust,
    down our long gravel road.

I remember the first time I drove our car
    with the neighbor gal, but I didn't get far.
Underneath the shining summer stars,
    on our long gravel road.

Our neighbor kid had gone to war,
    my mom told me he wouldn't be back no more.
The old folks gathered at the country store,
    on our long gravel road.

Down our gravel road, the world spun round,
    it was all I knew it was, all I found.
To me it was just Solomon ground,
    that long gravel road.

The mud was thick and the driving slow,
    when the rains poured down and the wind would blow.
But I really had no place to go,
    but down our long gravel road.

I remember when my sister moved away,
  my mom stood there with not much to say.
I just watched her car as it faded away,
  down our long gravel road.

One day the County trucks pulled in,
  black-topped our road from end to end.
Progress had shown its ugly hand,
  on our long gravel road.

Now life has changed one more time.
  My dad told me it would be just fine,
But I feel that I left my life behind,
  on our long gravel road.

Now the life I'm living could use a change,
    slow down a bit, maybe rearranged.
Think I will buy me a house on the open range,
    with a long gravel road.

Gravel roads have a way of changing you
    to the way of life that is pure and true.
Head back to a life that I once knew
    down a long gravel road.

If you have a reason to look for me,
    I live in the house that you can barely see
Down a long gravel road lined with trees.
    I think I'm home, back where I belong, on a long gravel road.

A Taste Of Our Past

They say that taste can take ya to a time that you once knew—
The taste of ice cream from a churn at the back yard barbecue.

Fresh corn bread a cookin' in your mom's old country stove:
Fresh corncobs, a big pot roast and good old buttered rolls.

Long green beans and bacon is a combo from my youth.
Lemon pie with meringue stacked high does fill my sweet tooth.

Jerky from a smoke house, that brine I remember well.
Sausages frying in a pan, I just love that ol' time smell.

Fried chicken stacked on paper plates, I'd quickly take my seat.
Ice cream on good ol' apple pie, would make my day complete.

Home made wine and home made beer would be put to the test.
But I think that homemade root beer is the very best.

Pork chops frying in a pan, the grease would splash so high.
Angel cake would rise so fast, never knew the reason why.

Whipping cream in a mixing bowl, add some sugar just for taste.
Strawberries on shortcake, whipped cream smeared on your face.

French toast and big ol' pancakes, maple syrup from a tree.
Back in the good ol' days is where I long to be.

But there is one taste I will remember until my dying days.
The taste of that damn sour milk will never go away.

Mountain Prayer

The beauty is vast beneath you
   with the colors that run deep.
The paint horse bows his head
   respecting natures dignity.

You wonder if the Indians
   took time to take it in
With all of nature at their feet.
   If not, it was a sin.

Who could miss the mountain flowers
   colored with fall gold.
Rock cliffs and the wind-burnt trees
   have a story that needs told.

You wonder why this ol' horse's head
   is bending, oh, so low.
Maybe it's spirits from years gone past,
   a sense he truly knows.

Just imagine two hundred years ago
   what this country was.
This virgin land teaching warriors
   to stop and calmly pause.

You can see how all the spirits
   came into the natives' lives.
Now it's you and a painted pony
   standing on that mountain side.

The Gathering

No matter what you think you are,
    it is so much more than you.
It outweighs all that you have done
    and all that you pursue.

A silence that takes everything
    and makes time just slip away.
The paint horse bows his head
    as if he knew to pray.

Soon the skies will darken
    and the air will turn to ice.
Snow will fall, the wind will call
    from morning through the night.

Spirits chase you down the hill
    from this beauty that you've found.
Mountain flowers will bow their heads
    then lay upon the ground.

A few men have tried to stay to fight
    the winter with their pride.
When their pride had given up
    they just fought to stay alive.

Maybe there's an understanding,
    that this horse has come to share.
You kneel down beside him
    to say a little mountain prayer.

Photo by Sharon Buol

Mike Whitaker and Paul Buol enjoying the mountains

Rockin' Diamond G
Outfitters

Rockin' Diamond G

It was early summer. The snow was still low,
  a few more weeks 'til it melted away.
I drove up the hill to an empty corral,
  blue skies, a barn the color of gray.

Just a bit early for any horse trips.
  It was quiet, couldn't hear a sound.
But I sat there for hours, the mountains I scoured,
  skipped rocks across the dusty ol' ground.

She's Grand Central Station when the summer sun shines,
  but for now she is quiet as can be.
The folks that own her love the life that they live
  here at the Rockin' Diamond G.

The Rockin' Diamond G sits all by herself
  at the foot of tree covered hills.
It's a dream that came true of a life they pursued,
  nice life for Lauri and Bill.

The ol' saddle racks that sit, oh, so empty,
  will be full in a short while.
The corrals will be full with horses and mules.
  They'll soon cover many a mile.

The people will arrive to have the time of their lives.
  The trips will start once again.
But I sit here today watchin' weathered trees sway
  just hatin' to see this day end.

Most folk don't like quiet, to be all alone,
    but a quiet place works just fine for me.
I think I'll sit a spell longer, I have a few things to ponder,
    just me and the ol' Rockin' Diamond G.

She smells like ol' leather, the barn is now weathered.
    The corrals are dusty and dry.
The mountains are stunning, the cold creeks are running.
    The sun now fills up the blue sky.

Well, I best get on going, the night air is showing.
    The ol' wind is pushin' hard on the trees.
Now I'd have to say, it's been a nice afternoon stay,
    just me and the ol' Rockin' Diamond G.

To Bill and Lauri Gallion, thank you for all that you've done.
Bill, I'm sure glad you stopped by for that cup of coffee.
We both have always said that change is good.
Had no idea it would be this good.

"Them Ol' Cowboy Days"

G   Am
An ol' crusty cowboy who lived off the land,
  D7   G
My gran'daddy raised me in the state of Montan.
         Am
Herdin' the cattle when I was just three,
  D7   G
My dog, my pony, my grand dad and me

D7   G
Yippee ci yi yea my gran'dad would sing.

            D7
He'd yip and he'd holler at round up each spring,
G   Am
Herdin' the cattle and chasin' the strays.
  D7   G
I dream of Montana and them ol' cowboy days.

Am
Our camp cook was Andy, he had western charm.
   D7   G
He'd cook up them fixin's with only one arm.
        Am
Stack them Dutch ovens clear up to the sky.
D7   G
Best gol darn cook and I'm tellin' no lie.

D7   **G**
Yippee ci yi yoo my gran'dad would sing.

                                                    D7
He'd hoot and he'd holler at round up each spring,
G   **Am**
Herdin' the cattle and chasin' the strays.
   D7   **G**
I dream of Montana and them ol' cowboy days.

Am
My gran'dad's been gone now for thirty some years.
         D7   **G**
When I think about him I fight them ol' tears.
Am
I still hear him beller on a lovely spring day
         D7   **G**
As I herd the cattle and chase them ol' strays.

      D7   **G**
Yippee ci yi yea my gran'dad would sing.

                                        D7
He'd yip and he'd holler at round up each spring
G   **Am**
Herdin' the cattle and chasin' the strays.
   D7   **G**
I dream of Montana and them ol' cowboy days.

Am
Now I am an old man and I still reminisce.
     D7   **G**
Those days in Montana I truly do miss.
                              Am
A one-armed camp cook and my gran'dad so dear,
  D7   **G**
I still think about them at round up each year

D7   **G**
Yippee ci yi yoo my gran'dad would sing.
                             D7
He'd yip and he'd holler at round up each spring
G   **Am**
Herdin' the cattle and chasin' the strays.
  D7   **G**
I dream of Montana and them ol' cowboy days.

  D7   **G**
I dream of Montana and them ol' cowboy days.

Lingerin' Memories

Up the side of this over-grown hill,
    over Scouts Pass and then down to the lake.
Mountain flower prettier than any ol' picture
    that a man would dare to take.

Found us a spot to string up the tent,
    unloaded the horses one more time.
Built us a fire as the evening retires,
    headed out to see what wood I could find.

Fished for a day, then my ol' man got restless.
    The next day we went on our way.
Didn't know exactly where we were goin';
    a surprise is all that the ol' man would say.

I bet ya I was only twelve years old,
    and to me bein' there was a dream.
Blue skies, blue lakes, cliffs as tall as forever,
    mountain meadows and cold running streams.

We'd been ridin' a spell, my backside was real sore,
    and how much longer was on my mind.
My ol' man would smile and say, "Two or three miles.
    Boy, you are one of a kind."

Came cross this meadow and just lying there
    was a plane or what was left of it.
All I could think of was I was glad I wasn't on her,
    must of hurt when the old girl hit.

Then the old man just stopped and looked side to side.
    I wondered what he was lookin' for.
A grin covered his face. He looked back at me
    and said, "Kind of hard to find the front door."

We fought through the brush to a meadow so green,
    and standin' in the sunshine
A cabin of old and a sign over her door
    that read, "Arrow Head Mine."

I walked on inside, she was just like a temple—
    bunks and a big ol' wood stove,
Pots and pans, shelves loaded with food;
    fell in love with this cabin of old.

We settled on in, made us some supper,
    then went for a look around.
My ol' man looked up to the hills around us.
    My eyes were searchin' the ground.

We heard some horses bustin' through the brush.
    Then a "Howdy" came through the air.
My ol' man did chuckle. See, it was just some old friends
    he hadn't seen in quite a few years.

The man and his wife were really nice folk.
    They seemed to take a likin' to me.
That night by the fire I just sat and listened,
    the folks sharin' old memories.

I woke the next morning to sizzlin' bacon,
    pancakes and eggs cooked just right.
I'm not sayin' that the ol' man had a hard time at cookin',
    but I'm glad that Bob brought his wife.

As the sun started to warm the meadow was showin' her charm.
    We packed up for the long ride out.
Shared the ride with the Marstens on that hot summer day.
    Ya know what I was dreamin' about.

The cabin's long gone, see, some overthinkers,
    somehow thought she just didn't belong.
I'll never forget that night at the cabin
    where memories just linger on,
        and on.

Photo by Lauri Gallion

To my dad and the days at Arrowhead

A Cowboy of Old

On a cool summer's evenin' by an open campfire
    my uncle sits all alone.
I found me a spot right next to him,
    smiled and asked him, "What's going on?"

He pushed up the brim of his old Cowboy hat
    far above those tired ol' eyes.
He seemed to have questions from way deep within.
    He got quiet and stared at that fire.

Now he wonders if he is a Cowboy,
    the kind from way long ago.
A Cowboy that rides clear cross the mountains
    and valleys of old Idaho.

He wonders if he is a Cowboy,
    if he could have made the grade.
Could he measure up to those ol' time Cowboys?
    He just sits with nothin' to say.

Dusty old boots, a hat stained with sweat,
    and a look that everyone knows.
That wore-out old hat that sits on his head
    is a friend from way long ago.

The way he handles the horses,
    the way he lives his life.
He lives his life that old Cowboy way
    with a distant look in his eyes.

He knows that he is a Cowboy,
    the kind from way long ago.
A cowboy that rides from here to forever,
    in the mountains of old Idaho.

He knows that he is a Cowboy,
    that he could've made the grade.
Measured up to those ol' time cowboys
    back in the hard drivin' days.

He's rode a lot horses.
    The mountains are his home.
He's packed them ol' mules for millions of miles.
    Together this land they've roamed.

Now we sit and stare at the fire.
    I don't know just what to say.
But I know he is a Cowboy,
    the kind from the ol' time days.

But he wonders if he is a Cowboy,
    the kind from way long ago.
A Cowboy that rides clear cross the mountains
    and valleys of old Idaho.

He wonders if he is a cowboy,
    if he could have made the grade.
Could he measure up to those old time Cowboys?
    He just sits with nothin' to say.

On a cool summer's evenin' by an open campfire,
    my uncle sits all alone.

On Occasions

I've been known to simply drag up
   and head down my own trail.
Float around like a maple leaf
   when the autumn winds prevail.

I really can't explain it
   or ever had the notion to.
It's not a cause, it's just a simple pause
   from the life that I pursue.

Just on an occasion
   seems I have to clear my mind.
Go to a simple place
   where the harvest moon does shine.

High in the back country
   where nature takes its course.
Ridin' high against the mountain sky,
   just me and my ol' horse.

Just on an occasion
   I'll be gone for quite a spell.
Where the lakes are blue, my headings true,
   where I land only time will tell.

The only rule at 6,000 feet
   is to let my conscience guide.
So I think I'll load my pony
   and head for a mountain ride.

Just on an occasion
    when I'm really not myself.
When I become a little ornery
    I find the feelings I once felt.

The feeling of a big ol' trout
    just tuggin' at my line.
Just sittin' by an ol' camp fire
    on a cool autumn night.

Don't think of me as reckless,
    untrustworthy or a case.
Just think of me as a simple man
    just travelin' at my own pace.

But on an occasion,
    when the autumn skies are blue.
I'll be ridin' my ol' pony
    on a course that's long and true.

The Carver

He digs through a pile of scrap and finds the perfect piece.
Builds a fire and finds a chair with an old dog at his feet.
He sits by the wood stove and he whittles at his wood.
It's an art that does take patience and is not exactly understood.

To think he takes a simple block and makes it come to life.
He holds it in his hands. There is amazement in his eyes.
I wonder what he is thinking with every swipe of his old knife.
His glasses sit upon his nose and he holds a steady eye.

He finishes the handy work and holds it in the air.
Its beauty fills up the moment; he pretends he doesn't care.
The way he sweeps the shavings and throws them in the fire.
Lends thought that he is satisfied, his day has now retired.

Sitting in the dark of the room is a carving of a dove.
Just a reminisce of an old man and the simple life he loves.
Most do not even know he has these gifts to bear.
Not sure why he doesn't show them or why he doesn't share.

But on the shelves that line the room are gifts from this old man.
Someday someone will find them, when his life comes to an end.
I could tell he was a carver, a sure and patient man.
I could tell he was an artist; he has a steady hand.

He's lived his life a quiet man, never had a lot to show.
I knew he was a carver, a man I'd like to know.
His time on earth is nearly gone, but he sits there in his chair.
His art is at its very best with none that can compare.

The many years he's worked, perfecting his fine trade.
All that will be left behind are the carvings that he's made.
But when he dies I'll lay at his side that perfect turtle dove.
Knowing he was a carver, a life he truly loved.

To Jim "God Bless"

Whiskey Friday Night

His old white barn hides in the dark.
   He makes his way inside.
He chops some wood and kindlin',
   loads it up and starts a fire.

The milk parlor he converted,
   into a meetin' room.
He grabs a broom to clean 'er up.
   They'll all be comin' soon.

Sweeps the dust into a pile,
   sweeps it in an old dust pan.
Stove gets hot, he turns 'er down,
   a bit more then he can stand.

Through the window he can see a truck
   comin' up the drive.
Friends supportin' a tradition,
   it's "Whiskey Friday Night."

Now "Whiskey Friday Night"
   sounds just a little stiff.
It's just honest folks a meetin',
   discussin' how they live.

It's but just a handful,
   of friends that come on by.
They can't remember when it started,
   or the reason why.

They talk about the cattle,
    the auction the next day.
The wives they talk of family,
    about that child that's on its way.

Photo by Air Photo, Inc.

The boys do have a snort or two,
    but it usually ain't real bad.
They talk of an old friend that passed on,
    the conversation does turn sad.

But they just get together,
    not a cross word or a fight.
It's a time when they slow down a bit.
    It's "Whiskey Friday Night."

They plan the next trip into the hills—
    they like their ridin' mules.
The women sometimes think they're silly,
    sometimes just damned ol' fools.

A compromise that they can live with,
    it lets the boys think they're right.
The gals know it means a lot to them,
    it's "Whiskey Friday Night."

It's a place where others come on by
    and share a thing or two.
It's a place where you can have a drink,
    talk of things that you pursue.

They tell their jokes and laugh out loud,
    The "BS" gets a little higher.
They shake their heads and chuckle,
    but wouldn't call a friend a liar.

The old white barn hides in the dark.
    These folks are feelin' right.
They throw another log upon the fire.
    It's "Whiskey Fire Day Night."

To the folks who gather on "Whiskey Friday"

There is an area outside of the small town of Enumclaw, Washington that is comprised of mostly second-generation dairy families. These folks are a pretty tight knit group. They are folks that help each other, share equipment and most importantly, share their lives.

There is an old white barn that once was used for milking but now is used for somethin' a little more special. See, on Friday nights there is an open invitation to drop by the barn and meet with all of the friends and neighbors. Usually fifteen to twenty folks will show up and simply talk of life and its adventures. It's a place where you can plan the next pack trip with their mules, talk of beef prices, milk prices, the new baby in the family or even announce a wedding.

But the most interestin' part of this tradition is its name. Somewhere along the line it became known as "Whiskey Friday." This poem is dedicated to that tradition and the folks that support it. So, when you're in our neck of the woods, swing by and say howdy. But don't forget to bring your own.

Standin' Proud and Tall

This here's a story I must share—
  a tale of no compare.
But first of all folks, my pard's a real square man.

But today I have some questions.
  It's a bit hard for me to mention.
See, sometimes a Cowboy has to take a stand.

See, we were getting' gussied up,
  headin' to Stockmen's for a cup.
Then I ran into a small dilemma.

My pard was feelin' good about himself,
  when he reached upon that shelf
And pulled down a blazin' pink bandana.

Fear ran through my eyes,
  but not a man to criticize,
I turned and looked him straight right in the eye.

I said, "Are you really wearing that?
  It don't even match your hat."
I was shootin' for a little compromise.

He turned and stared at me
  with his pride and dignity
And that pink bandana wrapped around his neck.

I said "We best get goin'."
  I guess my ignorance was showin'.
As we headed out I muttered, "What the heck."

Photo by Michael Whitaker

To my ol' pard Morry, man enough to wear a pink bandana.

He strolled her right inside,
   I held back so I could hide,
Tryin' to make some gol darn sense of this.

This gal said, "I like your scarf."
   It was then I nearly barfed,
And went into a hyperventilated fit.

A few Cowboys gave an eye,
   when my ol' pard meandered by,
And I knew this night was gonna be a dandy.

He ordered up a soda and a lime.
   I asked for the strongest whiskey they could find,
And I downed her like she was liquid candy.

An hour or two the went by
   and in the corner of my eye.
I saw a mountain of a man headin' our way.

I'm here to tell ya friends,
   I knew this was the end.
I'd be lucky if I saw another day.

Now this man that was so grand,
   he too was a pink bandana man.
I sat there dumbfounded and confused.

They talked of silk and slides,
   I darn near up and cried
And promptly ordered two more shots of booze.

That big man looked at me,
    said, "If you're secure with your masculinity,
The color pink don't matter much at all.

"I'm here to tell ya son,
    if you're packin' the right gun,
You'll be a cowboy standin' proud and tall."

Well, It started to make me think.
    What's with the color pink?
It's just another color in the sky.

But I've notice you all starin',
    at this ear ring that I'm wearin'.
Now I hope you understand the reason why.

Photo by Gwen Henson

Cow Camp

I'm usually not a sentimental man;
    usually not this way.
But if you could just indulge me, folks,
    I've got a few words I'd like to say.

See, I'm what you'd call a "greenhorn,"
    a new hire to this Camp.
Come here not knowing very much,
    I'm glad they took the chance.

First time I've been to Cow Camp.
    Somehow it seems so strange.
Ridin' horses for days on end
    across the open range.

But it turns out that these are real good folk,
    the kind that stands up tall.
They took good care of a "greenhorn" like me.
    I know I owe them all.

When I first showed up at Cow Camp
    they had this other hand.
He really didn't have a lot to say.
    He was a quiet man.

But Cowboy Skip could really sing
    around the fire each night.
But one morning he just drug up,
    rode his horse plumb out of sight.

Next to the ol' Chuck Wagon there
   is dear ol' Padre Gregg.
He's the cook of this here Cow Camp.
   He usually pulls your leg.

But knowin' that a Holy Man
   is cookin' just the same
Makes a Cowboy feel much better,
   out on the open range.

There, sitting right beside him,
   is Carla his dear wife.
Her trade is hitching horsehair.
   She works at it day and night.

The boys can somehow get to me.
   Sometimes they are a pain.
She'll sit and listen patiently
   As I moan and complain.

There stands Cowboy Keven.
   He can make you cry.
He talks about important things,
   the reasons and the whys.

He tells ya how it really is,
   just what you should do.
But, like the other Cowboys,
   he'll pull your leg an inch or two.

That Cowboy there we call old Spiff.
   To most he's known as Morry.
He is purt' near funny most all the time
   with each and every story.

He'll make you laugh 'til you can't breath.
    You'll just shake and shiver.
Then he'll stop you right dead in your tracks
    with the one from Snowy River.

Now Alan is the Honcho.
    He's the boss of this here Camp.
He's the one I owe the most to.
    He's the one that took the chance.

I met him singing by a mountain fire.
    That was a few years ago.
I'd have to say that this is the man
    that I truly owe.

Now, boys, the cattle are sold off,
    Our work here is now done.
I'm glad I got to know ya,
    each and everyone.

I enjoyed the verse you shared with me,
    the way ol' Alan sings.
But for now it's adios, my friends,
    I'll see ya at round up in the spring.

The photo below is of the Tahoma Range Rhymers (With Guest Appearance by Skip Gorman) and the poem is about each and everyone of them. These folks gave me the nudge and helped me get out there and recite the poems I wrote. I can't say enough about the kindness and patience these folks have shown towards me. I will always be indebted.

Photo by Melinda Walter

To (L to R) Alan Halvorson, Skip Gorman, Keven Inman, Carla and Gregg McDonald, and Morry Walters.

Photo by Nick Whitaker

Mike Whitaker, Cowboy Poet

Well, I live in a small town called Buckley, Washington. Buckley's located in the foothills of the Cascade Mountains and is a stones throw way from Mt. Rainier. Enjoy the out doors and can't get enough time in the high country. Buckley used to be a remote community, but like a lot of small towns now a days, we can see it comin'. Might have to head up the trail a bit farther to keep my sanity.

When I look back at my family's history and glance at old family pictures, there is one constant, the horse. The horse and the old ways have intrigued me ever since I was little. The cowboy life just has somethin' about it that just seems right. This tradition is still alive and well in our family and it looks as though it will be here for generations to come.

Some folks may think that I'm a recluse. On one of those rainy days when you can put the chores off for a spell, I just build me a fire in the wood stove out in the barn, sit in my rockin' chair and jot down a line or two. Oh ya have to put up with the typical

251

interruptions, such as the dogs leavin' the door open, but ya always have to put up with sacrifices.

As for my poetry, like many other writers, I've been writin' in one form or another all my life. Can't put my finger on why I write, but truly enjoy explorin' a thought now and then. I like to capture a real life experience and try to present it in a way that it makes folks reflect or at least think a bit. Since I've started doing poetry, each year has some how gotten bigger and bigger. I like doin' my poems and seein' the reaction from folks. It's funny, there have been many times that a person has walked up and said "What's Cowboy Poetry?" Those folks that ask this question are usually the ones that come up after the show and go on and on.

I guess I really didn't get to who I am or maybe I have. To explain who I am is real simple. See, my wife bought this cheesy framed quilted picture thing that is proudly hung from our living room wall and it simply reads,

"Country Music Hummed Here!" I guess that's who I am.

Order Form

❏ Yes! Please send me the following title.

Name_____

Address _____

City _____State _____Zip _____

Phone_____Fax _____

Title	Qty.	Each	Total
Cowboy Poetry, The Gathering. By Michael Whitaker. Foreword by Alan Halvorson.	_____	$19.95	_____
	Subtotal		_____
Please add $4.50 for the first item, plus $1.00 for each additional item for shipping and handling.	**S&H**		_____
Foreign orders must be accompanied by a postal money order in U.S. funds.	**TOTAL**		_____

Send check or money order to:
Mike Whitaker
12757 Pioneer Way E
Buckley, AZ 98321

To order by phone call (360) 829-2387 or email windyword@msn.com.
Contact us about discounts.